The Ashford Book of
Needle Felting

Inspirational Projects Stretching the Boundaries of Needle Felting

Barbara Allen

Contents

Introduction	3
Materials and equipment	4
Techniques and tips	7
Project 1 – Butterfly brooch	12
Project 2 – Child's jersey	16
Project 3 – Teddybear	22
Project 4 – Vest	32
Project 5 – Danish pastry	38
Project 6 – Tote bag	46
Project 7 – Iris blooms	52
Project 8 – French street scene	58
Project 9 – Camel	66
Project 10 – Poppies	80
Project patterns	90
Gallery	96

All rights reserved. No part of this publication may be reproduced, stored in a retrieval system or transmitted in any form by any means electronic, mechanical, photocopying, recording or otherwise, without prior permission from the publisher.

© 2008 Ashford Handicrafts Ltd

ISBN: 978-0-9582881-2-5
Printed in China by Everbest Ltd
Published by Ashford Handicrafts Ltd
Ashburton, New Zealand
Email: sales@ashford.co.nz

Photo art direction Tina Gill
Photography Tina Gill, Barbara Allen

Introduction to needle felting

Needle felting is a wonderful, relatively new craft, which has rapidly increased in popularity because it is easy to learn and allows endless possibilities for both flat and 3-dimensional work. The materials needed are few and relatively inexpensive, making this craft within reach of most people.

This form of dry felting can be taken to any level, from simple children's projects to a piece of fine art. Although the felting needle has been used commercially for about 100 years, it is only recently that fibre artists have begun using just one of these needles to create detailed projects in felt, from flat wall hangings to 3-dimensional animals and people.

The felting needle has tiny barbs near the tip that will grab hold of some fibres when you push the needle into a wad of wool. When you pull the needle out again, the fibres are left entangled where you pushed them. Felt is formed when the fibres are entangled together so tightly that they cannot be pulled apart. Traditionally this has been done with wet felting methods, using soap, water and friction to entangle the fibres. In dry needle felting it is the felting needle that entangles the fibres, so no water is needed. By using just one needle, we have far more control over where the wool is placed, and can form very intricate designs. We are, in effect, sculpting with wool!

This book will introduce you to the craft of needle felting and the equipment needed. Then it will take you on a journey from simple to more advanced projects, each one building on what you have learnt in the previous project. By the time you have worked through the book, you will be experienced and confident enough to create your own masterpieces. I hope the projects in the Gallery pages will then inspire you, and tempt you to reach further in your own creative endeavours.

Projects

As you begin to work through these ten projects you will quickly realise how easy needle felting is, and what amazing and rewarding results you can achieve with the use of such a simple tool. There are no rules with this craft; you can work with a single needle or several needles in a needle punch, the creation can be softly felted or very firm, flat or 3-dimensional. The possibilities are limited only by your imagination!

In this book I have used various backing fabrics for the flat felted projects. You can felt onto many surfaces, including commercial felt (either acrylic or wool), polar fleece, knitted garments and most kinds of woven fabrics like cotton or denim.

When making 3-D felted pieces, they can be felted wool all the way through, or they can have some sort of support inside, with needle felting used on the outside layers. The support inside can be wire wrapped with wool or polyester batting, or a stitched and stuffed fabric shape (eg. a teddybear or dog).

Flat felting and 3-D felting can be combined in the one piece, illustrated by the Noah's Ark wall hanging, which has some 3-D faces protruding from the surface, while others are flat.

You can also create fine shading from one colour to another, as in the Poppies picture, or the Mother and Baby picture in the Gallery.

Your projects can be embellished with embroidery and beadwork, as in the Tote bag and the Camel, even ribbons or lace.

Throughout the projects I have described the techniques and included various tips and these are all repeated in the Techniques and tips chapter so that you can refer to them easily.

It is a good idea to read through each project before you begin so that you understand how the work will progress. For each project I have listed all the materials you need. You will find patterns for the ten projects in the back of the book. They are also available on the Ashford's website as downloadable PDFs. To obtain the access code for the patterns please email sales@ashford.co.nz.

Materials and equipment

The main items for needle felting are felting needles, a foam block for a work base, and wool sliver or tops. These are described below, and I have also mentioned several other items that I find useful, though not strictly necessary.

Needles

Felting needles have no hole in the end to take a thread of cotton. Instead they have a short right-angle bend at the top, and the lower part of the shaft contains a blade with tiny barbs that point downwards and hook the fibres when you push into the wool. The needles are extremely sharp and come in a variety of sizes and types, ranging from coarse to very fine.

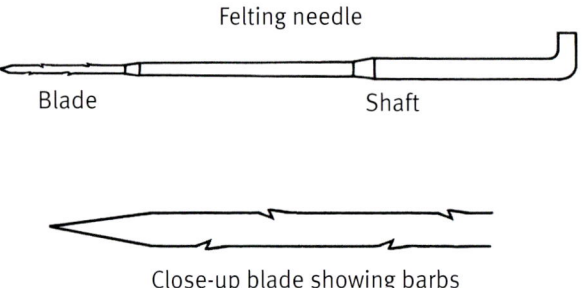

Size of needle: There are many different sized needles available. Some have a triangular blade (T) and some a star-shaped blade (S). The 'T' needles are good basic needles, and range in size from 32T to 42T, the larger the number the finer the needle. For deep penetration the barbs are spaced evenly up the length of the blade, but for shallow work (e.g. flat felting or surface finishing on 3-D projects) you can get needles with the barbs clustered close to the tip.

Star (S) needles have four indented sides, with barbs on all four edges. They make a smaller hole than their 'T' counterparts, and generally have barbs clustered closer to the tip. They are great for fine work, and are extremely good with Merino wool.

A medium needle (36T) is great for starting 3-dimensional projects and felting them down quickly, but I change to a fine needle (usually 38S or 40T) once the felt firms up a little. I prefer to use a fine needle (38S) for all my flat felting projects.

Using the needle correctly: The felting needle is made of mild steel, not tempered steel like normal sewing needles. Because of this the felting needle will snap if you put any sideways force on it as you work. The finer the needle the more easily it will snap if you try to push it sideways. This said, once you have a feel for felting you will rarely break a needle; it is only while you are beginning that you may snap a few.

Do be very careful with these needles, as they are sharp. Hold your needle with one hand and your wad of wool with the other, fingers on each side of the wad resting on the foam pad. You may find it comfortable to slide your index finger down the shaft of the needle until it is about 2.5cm (1in) from the tip, so that you can feel roughly how close the tip is to your other hand. When you are learning, watch closely where the needle is going and don't be tempted to look away while you work.

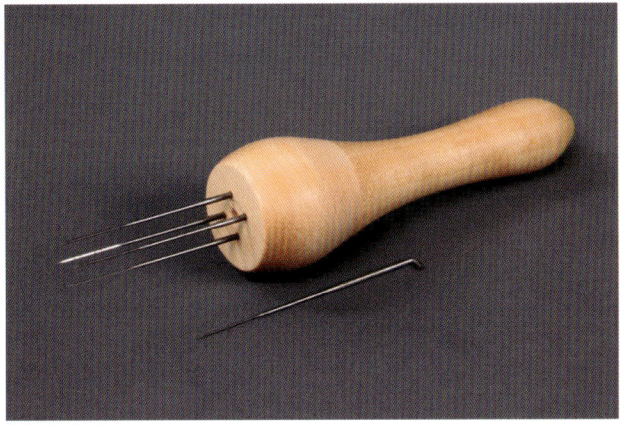

Needle punches: Needle punches are tools with a handle that hold several needles at once, so that when you punch down, you have 3 – 5 needles entering your work at the same time. They are ideal when working a flat felted picture or a large 3-D project, as they will firm the surface a lot faster than if you were only using a single needle.

Water soluble stabiliser

In most flat felted projects I have used **water-soluble stabiliser** to transfer a pattern. This is a non-woven, soft, paper-like fabric, and comes in several different brands, like Vilene® and Wash Away, so I will refer to it throughout the book as 'stabiliser'. You can trace your pattern onto this, cut it out and pin to the backing fabric. The wool can be needle felted directly on to it, so that you can see exactly where you want the wool to go. Once the project is finished, a quick rinse in warm water will dissolve the stabiliser. You can also leave it in place if it is completely covered by your needle felting.

Water soluble marker pen

This is a useful pen for drawing your patterns, and when a project is finished if there is any marker still showing it can be removed with a damp brush or a drop of water, just like the stabiliser. You can still use a fine ordinary pen if you don't have a water soluble one, just don't make the lines too thick.

Soft brush

When working on clothing items, you may find that stray wool fibres settle on the surrounding fabric. I have found a good way to remove these is with a soft rubber-bristled pet hair brush. Simply sweep the brush over the fabric (not the needle felting) and it will pick up all these fibres and leave the fabric clean.

Foam block

You need to have a soft base under your work and I find foam to be the best option. A foam block 13cm (5ins) square and 5cm (2ins) thick is suitable for most 3-D work and some smaller flat work. However, if you are making a large flat-felted picture you will need a large piece of foam, preferably slightly bigger than the picture.

Fibre

For needle felting we use the same type of fibre that a spinner would use when spinning yarn. There is a great variety of fibres suitable for needle felting, from wool to angora, alpaca, silk fibres, camel or even pet hair! I have even seen a project needle felted from polyester stuffing fibre! Some fibres felt more readily than others, but as a guide any fibre that is good for wet felting can be used to needle felt, such as Corriedale and Romney wool.

Commercially prepared wool is readily available for needle felting, either natural or dyed in many exciting colours. I find NZ Corriedale sliver great to use as it felts down easily and quickly. I also like using Merino sliver. Although it takes a little longer to felt down for 3-dimensional projects, it is very fine, and perfect for flat felting. Ashfords have a wonderful range of Corriedale, Merino and Alpaca Blend wools and in the project instructions I have listed the colours to use from their range.

Some of the Ashford range of wool slivers.

Techniques and tips

3-dimensional felting

Mixing fibres: By mixing the wool in your fingers before you start felting, the fibres will go in all different directions, not just in one direction, so that when the wool is needle felted, the fibres will hold together and not split apart, as they tend to do if the fibres are lying all in the same direction.

Compressing the wool: To cut down on felting time, compress the loose wool into a tight mass with one hand, while needle felting with the other. Squeezing the wool together means that there are more fibres in a smaller area, therefore your felting needle can pick up more of these fibres with its barbs at each stroke, making the felting process faster.

Another excellent method is to roll the wool into a tight ball or cylinder before beginning to work with the needle. The tighter you roll the quicker the felting process will be.

Correcting the shape: If you find that your work is not staying in the desired shape, work your needle into the areas that are bulging out of line, and they will go back in. This is how you control the shaping.

Resizing a piece: Sometimes the piece you are working on becomes too small as it felts down. This is very easy to fix by adding more wool and felting it in. Also, if a piece has been felted down firmly and is still too big (e.g. one arm longer than the other) simply take your scissors to it and cut the extra length off. Then round the cut edge over by trimming with scissors or by needling. You can 'skin' over this with a thin wisp of wool, to hide the cut edges if desired.

Needling edges between fingers: Firm up the edges of thin pieces like ears or eyelids by holding between your thumb and forefinger and carefully jiggling the needle in and out, working right around the edges. If you hold the piece deeply and not at the very tip of your fingers, you are less likely to prick yourself as the point of the needle does not need to be pulled out from between your fingers as you jiggle it. You will find this method works wonders at defining and firming up the edges.

Trimming: Trim your project with scissors once finished to get rid of any wispy fibres that have not been felted down.

Techniques and tips ... continued

Flat felting

Flat felting on foam base: When making a flat needle felted design, the fibres will become embedded in the foam work base underneath. It may be tempting to pull the work off the foam frequently to prevent embedding or to inspect the back, but I find it is best not to do this until the project is completely finished. If it is pulled off the foam and then laid back down so that you can continue to work, the fibres on the back will make bumps underneath which are difficult to work around.

When the project is completely finished, pull it off the foam SLOWLY, so that you don't rip the foam and leave too much of it attached to the back of your work. If there are still a few small pieces attached to the project, tease them out with a pin or a sewing needle (not a felting needle or you may break it).

Using multiple layers of stabiliser: Once you have needle felted over your stabiliser pattern, you can place another stabiliser pattern piece on top and needle felt over this as well. Using this method helps to define subsequent shapes as you build up your picture.

Length of fibres for flat felting: I like to work with fibres that are 2.5 – 5cm (1 – 2ins) long. These are mixed in my fingers before applying so the fibres run in all directions. Having short fibres like this helps prevent the unwanted effect of lines of fibre where I don't want them. It also makes it easier to pull off small amounts of felted wool from the piece if something needs correcting, without disturbing all the work around it.

When mixing colours for small areas use even shorter fibres. Having short fibres allows better blending in a small wad, and by using smaller wads of wool when filling in an area, you also have more control about where the wool is going. For larger areas, use longer fibres and bigger wads of wool.

Thickness of flat felt: Make your base layers of wool generous when flat felting; your finished work will look more vibrant than if the layer is thin and wispy. Of course once you have this base layer and you want to lay light shadows or colour changes on top, these subsequent layers may be fine and thin to allow the base colour to show through.

If you have a small area that appears to be lumpy and raised higher than the surrounding wool, keep needling this area to push the extra fibres through to the back of the project where they won't show. If, as you are needling your colour on, you feel there is too much wool in your wad, just pull some of it off. This is the beauty of working with fibres that are only short, if you need to pull some off, it will come away easily without disturbing too much of the surrounding work.

Blending wool colours: If you don't have the exact colour that you need for a project, blending is an ideal way to extend your colour range. I like to make the blending fibres about 2.5 – 3cm (1 – 1.5ins) long, then take small amounts of the colours required and mix them thoroughly in my fingers. If this is done properly it will be difficult to discern the mixed colours from the plain colours in the project. If you want an interesting marbled affect, don't mix them quite so thoroughly.

Tease out a small amount of fibres for your first colour and lay them on the foam. Lay your second colour on top, also teased out. Pick the wad up in your fingers, holding firmly between thumb and forefinger, then give a good tug with your other hand to pull a few wispy strands out of the side. Place these on the top of the wad, turn it clockwise a little, hold tight again and tug out another small amount. Keep turning, tugging and blending until you can no longer see the individual colours and the blend looks even. I find holding the wool firmly makes for a quicker blending than if you just fluff the wool lightly, backwards and forwards between both hands.

I also find that I get a better, faster blend if I mix small amounts at a time. This way I can see if the fibres of one colour have remained stuck together and need teasing out.

Making an edge: (A) Dent and fold method – When making a dented line for an edge, I use my fingernail to run the needle down to ensure the needle goes exactly where I want it to. If you are concerned about using your fingernail, you may be more comfortable using the end of a small teaspoon for curved edges, or a ruler for a straight edge. Once the edge is marked with a dent, you can fold over the excess wool and felt it down.

Denting with a ruler.

Blending wool colours.

With a teaspoon.

Techniques and tips ... continued

With a finger nail.

Folding the dent.

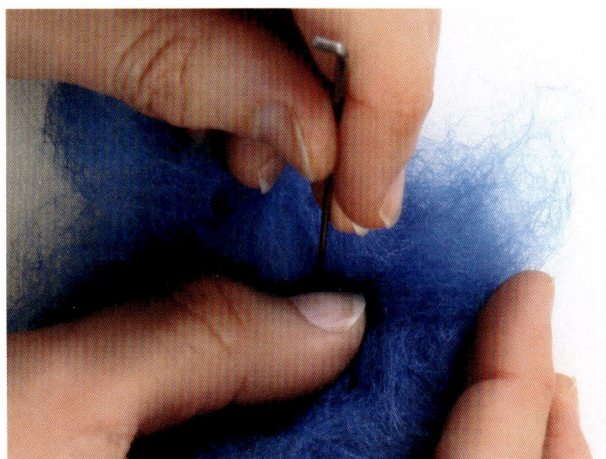

With a thumb nail.

(B) Fingernail facing method – Another method is to place your fingernail on the outer edge facing the work, and felt up to it. As you slide the needle gently up and down against your fingernail the wool will tuck in neatly just in front of it. You can't accidentally felt past where your fingernail is, so it gives you a well defined edge, without folding over the excess as in the method above.

Twirling the needle: To quickly catch the last few wispy fibres to felt down, twirl the needle around in a tiny circle just above the surface of the felt and this will catch the fibres, and then work them in. Repeat if necessary.

Smoothing the surface: The finer the needle you use, the smaller the holes are, so make sure you go over your work with your fine needle to finish the surface, and minimise holes. If you feel after you have finished your project that you can still see too many needle holes, gently rub the surface with your fingers and you will find that many of the holes are smoothed over.

Feathering edges: When adding more wool to a piece, tease out the edges as you work to hide the join. However, if you find that once the wool has been felted down there is a definite edge where the new wool meets the old, take your scissors and make several snips in the line of the wool, then tease the cut ends out so the line is no longer visible, and felt the loose fibres back down to blend them in to the background.

Removing the stabiliser: If any small edges of stabiliser are showing once you have finished a project and you do not want to wash the whole thing, use a stiff bristled paintbrush dipped in warm water and 'paint' the stabiliser away!

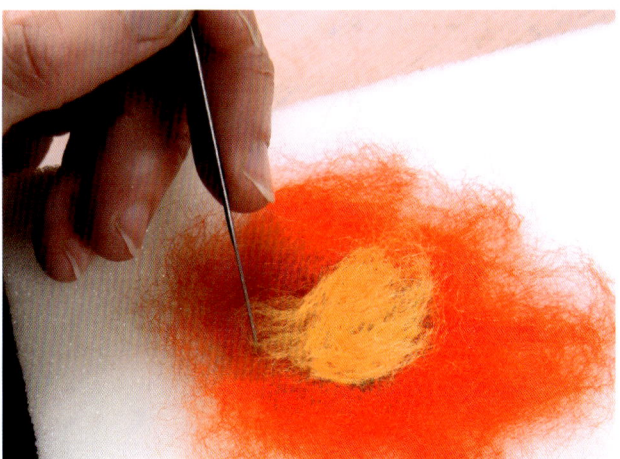

Feathering different colours: You can also use this feathering method if you find that you are getting a harsh line where two colours meet and you want to have a soft blending of one colour into the next.

Butterfly brooch
Project 1

This quick and easy flat felted brooch will give you a feel for how the felting needle works and you will have a bright, eye-catching brooch to wear. Once you have made a simple butterfly, you can experiment with more adventurous patterning on your next butterfly, to achieve even more striking effects.

You will need:
Merino wool sliver Tangerine 2gm ($1/16$oz),
Lagoon 2gm ($1/16$oz), Liquorice small piece
Black felt for backing (acrylic or wool)
Fine wire for antennae, painted black
Water soluble stabiliser
Brooch pin
Felting needle 38S

Finished size: 5.5cm ($2 1/4$ins) high

1. Trace the butterfly pattern onto the stabiliser fabric and cut out leaving a small margin around the edge. Cut a square of black felt a little larger than the pattern and pin them both to the foam.

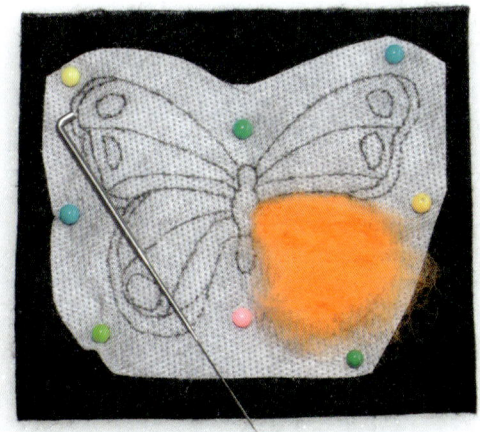

2. The wings: Work on the lower part of each wing first. Take a small wad of Tangerine wool, pull the fibres apart and mix them around with your fingers so that they are not all lying in the same direction. Shape the wool roughly to the size of one of the lower wings and hold it in place. Now push your fine felting needle (38S) through the wool until it goes into the foam underneath (it needs to go about $1/2$cm, or $1/4$in, into the foam). Pull the needle out and repeat. It is as easy as that! Now you are needle felting!

Needle all over the lower wing area, but stay inside the pattern. As you continue to work you will see the wool gradually felt down onto the backing fabric. Use your needle to gently move the fibres to get an even covering as you felt the wool into place. Add more wool if you find the covering is thin in some areas.

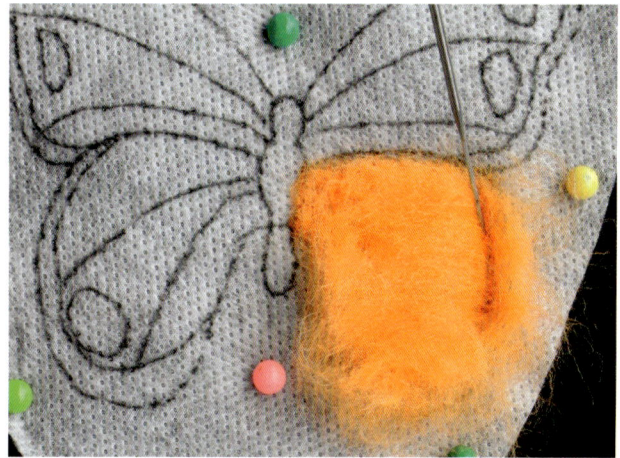

3. Remember to leave a small margin inside the edge of the wing. The black felt margin will look quite striking against the Tangerine wool when the stabiliser is removed later. To form a neat line at the edge of the Tangerine, make a row of dents close together along the line where the Tangerine meets the black edge of the wing. Now gently lift any loose fibres that are outside the line back over into the main Tangerine area and needle them down.

You will notice that as you needle felt, some of the fibres will be pushed down and embedded into the foam, so that the piece you are working on will become attached to the foam. In a flat project like this it doesn't matter, and we will peel the butterfly off the foam once it is finished.

Butterfly brooch ... continued

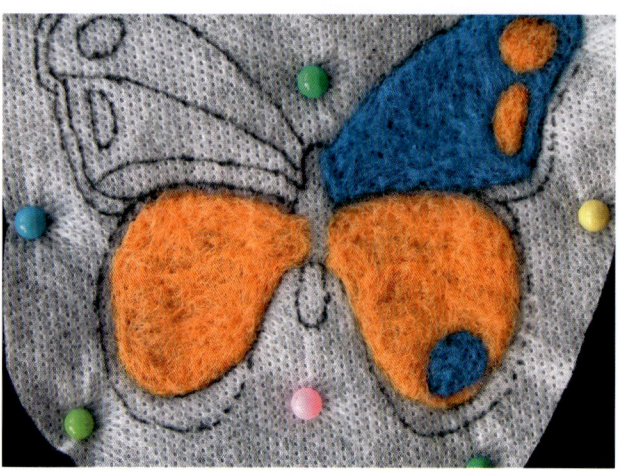

4. Felt the Tangerine wool firmly, then put a spot of colour on the lower wing. Take a tiny wad of Lagoon wool, mix it with your fingers and roll it into a loose ball, about the size of the spot. You want this to be flat, not raised above the rest of the surface when you have finished felting, so don't put too much wool into it. Needle the spot on to the Tangerine felt: no sewing involved to join colours, it is all done with the felting needle!

Continue to work into the spot, using the needle to gently persuade the wool to the shape that you want. You can use your fingernail as a guide to define where the edge of the wool is to be by placing it on the line. Slide the needle gently up and down against your fingernail and into the wool, and the needle will make a sharp line there. Neaten the edge as you did with the Tangerine edges, working until it is well defined.

5. Repeat the process for the other wing areas, using the photograph for reference. Leave a thin margin between the upper and lower wings, and when the stabiliser is washed away, it will leave a black line of the backing felt showing.

6. To make thin lines of contrasting colour, pull out a thin length of fibres from the main part of the wool, as a spinner would do if they were going to spin yarn. Give the fibres a twist and then lay them on the wing, starting at the body edge.

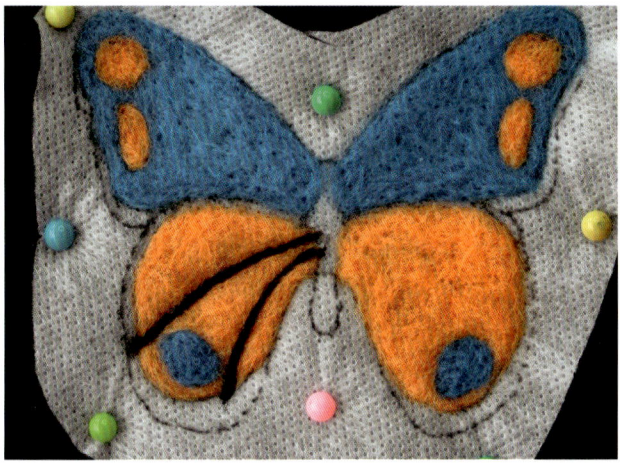

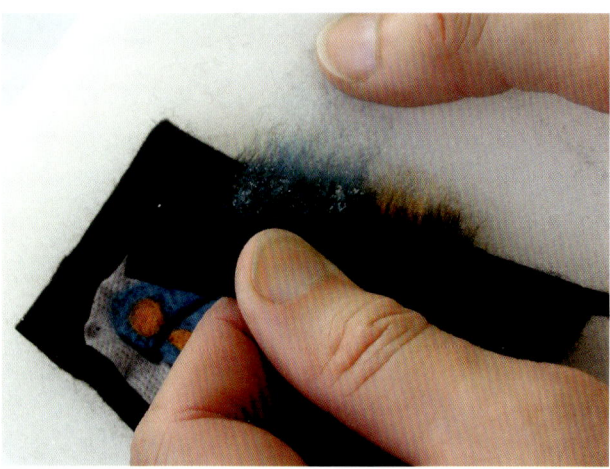

7. Needle the ends of the fibres until they are firmly attached, then lay the yarn down on the wing and continue working along the length of the wool until it is attached, curving it as needed.

9. Remove the butterfly from the foam by carefully pulling the backing felt away from the foam. You will be left with lots of wispy fibres on the wrong side of the butterfly.

8. When you get the to the other end, after attaching the rest of the line, cut the fibres off so that there is about ½cm (¼in) left longer than the desired length. Needle these ends repeatedly: they will gradually bury themselves in the felt and you will have a nice clean finish to the line of wool.

If you prefer, yarn can be used for the lines. You can add different colours to complement the colours you already have, or just use black for a strong contrast.

10. It is not a good idea to cut these off, as they are helping to attach the wool. If they bother you, take your felting needle and hold it on a slant almost parallel with the surface, then gently work at these fibres to push them back into the black felt backing. You don't want to push them right through to the other side though, that is why we need to use the needle on an angle. Cut the butterfly around the outline.

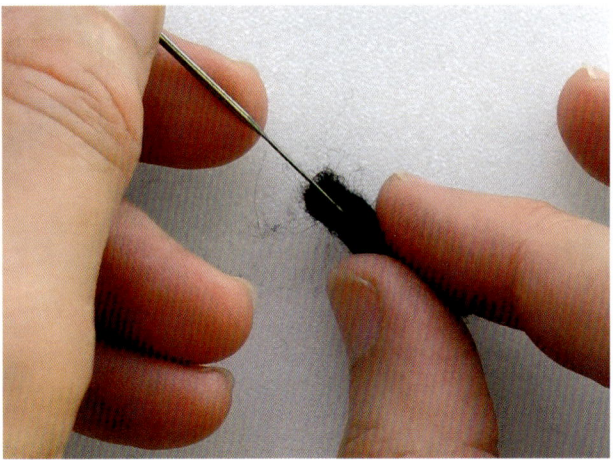

11. The body: Prepare the antennae by cutting your wire and bending it in half. Bend the ends over and shape the antennae in a nice curve. The wire can be painted with black paint, or coloured nail varnish for a bright effect.

For the body, shape a rough cylinder of Liquorice wool a little larger than the body will be when finished, as the wool will reduce in size as it felts. Place this on your foam block and needle to firm it up slightly. You don't want the body to attach to the foam at this point, as the wings did, so pick it up and turn it over several times as you needle it to prevent this happening. Use your needle in a sideways motion, working down the length of the body, instead of straight across the body, as this would cause a lot of loose fibres to stick out of the sides. The tail section will extend beyond the wings, so work this a little firmer than the rest of the body.

12. Position the body on the wings and needle felt to attach, allowing the finished shape to be a little rounded and not as flat as when you added the coloured spots.

13. Before attaching the head, slip the V part of the antennae between the wings and the head. Carefully needle around and through the head to attach it to the wings, at the same time sealing in the wire antennae. Work slowly so that you don't snap your needle on the wire. Continue to needle this area until the antennae are firmly attached.

14. The final touch is to bend the wings up slightly to make your butterfly come alive. Place it back on the foam and put your thumbnail along the line between the body and the wing on one side. Bend the wing up a little and needle along the body line to hold. Repeat for the other side.

Rinse your butterfly in warm water to dissolve the stabiliser fabric, then pat dry on a towel. Leave to dry then sew a brooch pin on the back, and there you have your finished butterfly, all ready to wear!

Child's jersey

Project 2

This project is needle felted onto a knitted woollen jersey, using stabiliser fabric for transferring the pattern. Once the needle felting is applied, if the jersey needs washing it should be hand washed, or machine washed on woollen cycle, to prevent the pictures felting too much more.

Although this train is felted onto a knitted jersey, it could be just as easily felted onto polar fleece. I am sure the train will delight some lucky little boy or girl!

You will need:
Merino wool sliver Scarlet 2gm ($^1/_{16}$oz),
Blueberry Pie 2gm ($^1/_{16}$oz), Beansprout 2gm ($^1/_{16}$oz),
Liquorice 1gm ($^1/_{32}$oz), White small piece
Corriedale wool sliver Lemon 1gm ($^1/_{32}$oz),
Kiwifruit 1gm ($^1/_{32}$oz)
Child's jersey
Water soluble stabiliser
Black embroidery cotton
Felting needle 38S

Finished size: 7.8cm (3ins) high

1. Begin by drawing the train and carriage on the stabiliser and cutting the pattern out, leaving a margin around the edge. Place a foam block inside the jersey and position the pattern so that it is sitting evenly on the front of the jersey. Pin the pattern on by pushing the pins down through the jersey and into the foam underneath.

Needle felt the front wheel that is partially hidden, using Liquorice wool, then work forward with your colours from there.

2. Because of the nature of a knitted garment, which will move and stretch as it is being worn, it is better to make a strong joint where two colours meet. You will need to run one colour underneath the next, so that if it stretches, the two colours won't pull apart. Continue to make clean sharp edges around the outside of the picture, as in the butterfly, but build the inner joints one on top of another.

3. To do this, let the lower colour (e.g. green) spread over the line where it joins the next colour (e.g. red). When you place the red beside it, make a sharp line where the original line was drawn on the pattern. This will reinforce the colour joins so that they won't pull apart.

4. When building up an area of colour, felt a small amount of wool on, then add another small wad and felt this beside the first. Continue like this until the whole area is filled. In this way you will have more control over where the wool goes and how much is used in each area. Once you have established the edges of a shape (using the dent-and-fold method or your fingernail), a needle punch tool will quickly felt down the wool within the shape. A single needle will do just as well; it merely takes a little longer.

If you find that you are losing track of where the edges are, because wool from a nearby colour is overlapping, try adding another piece of stabiliser with just the pattern for the shape you are working on, e.g. the black wheels.

These can be pinned directly on top of the previous pattern and felting, and will show you clearly where the edges are. Felt through all layers. Once you rinse out the stabiliser you won't know there was ever another layer put in there.

When you have a shape that comes to a sharp point, as in the front end of the wagon, roll the wad of wool between your fingers to form a sharp point before applying it to the design and felting it down. Felt the oval of the eyes with white wool, then add a smaller oval inside of black for the pupils.

5. Once the needle felting is complete, you may like to cut the surplus stabiliser from the design (although this is not really necessary as it will wash off), then pull the jersey carefully off the foam and turn it inside out. Needle the wispy fibres on the inside to work them back into the jersey, with your needle on a slant as you did on the butterfly.

6. Embroider the outlines around each shape using black embroidery cotton and stem stitch. Also embroider smoke coming out of the funnel, if desired.

Teddybear

Project 3

A teddybear is an easy project to make when learning 3-dimensional felting. This little bear measures about 10cm (4ins) tall when standing. His limbs and head are thread-jointed so that they can be moved, and he has glass teddybear eyes for a more realistic look. Use your medium needle (36T) when you start to needle the loose wool, and change to your fine needle (40T) once the felt has become firmer. I have used Corriedale wool for this teddy as it felts down easily and quickly.

You will need:
Corriedale wool sliver Peach 20gm ($3/4$oz), Skin 5gm ($1/8$oz),
Liquorice small piece
Glass teddy bear eyes 3mm ($1/8$in)
Dental floss for jointing
Thread for eyebrows and mouth
Long doll needle
Small pliers
Felting needles 36T, 40T

Finished size: 10cm (4ins) tall when standing

The pattern (on page 91) shows the basic teddy shapes that we are going to make. The small half circle is the ear. Use the shapes as a guide only, as you will find that your bear grows into an individual as you work.

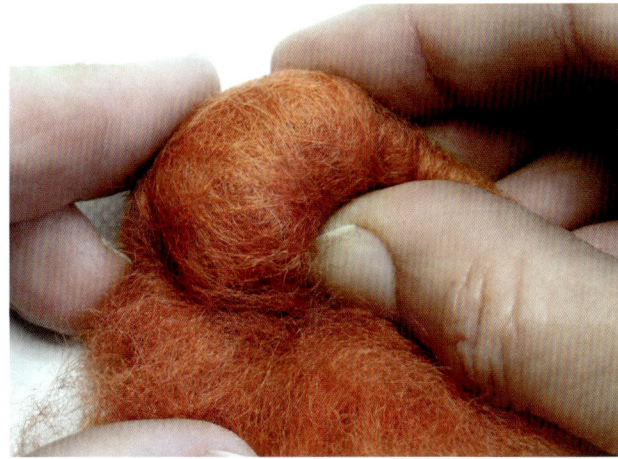

1. The head: Begin by making a ball-shape of Peach wool. To do this take a 12cm (5ins) length of wool, mix it in your fingers, then roll it up into a tight ball (rolling your wool tightly reduces the felting time). Needle the ball a few times with your 36T needle to stop it from unrolling. At this stage you need to insert your needle about 2.5cm (1in) deep into the wool. Change to a 40T when the 36T starts to resist being pushed into the felt. You may find that the surface becomes rather bumpy but don't worry about it, just needle the little bumps and avoid working the hollows too much and the surface will eventually even out. Continue needling all over the surface of the ball until it is firm and a nice round shape.

Tip: If you find that the ball is not staying in shape, work your needle into the areas that are bulging out of line, and they will go back in. This is how you control the shaping.

2. Make the muzzle with Skin wool, using about a quarter of the amount used for the main head. Using the same method as for the head, roll a short cylinder shape, and then needle until about half firm, remembering to work the ends as well as the middle. Make a dent in the middle, so that it is a kidney shape. The dent is where the nose will go. To form the dent, work a line across the top of the oval. Keep needling along this line until a dent forms, then smooth the edges around the dent by working them as well as working in the dent.

Teddybear ... continued

3. Attach the muzzle to the head, dent-side up, before the muzzle gets too firm, otherwise it will be hard to attach properly. Use the photos as a guide, and place the lower part of the muzzle (the curved side) at the bottom of the face where the chin will be. The rest of the muzzle should extend no further than half way up the face, preferably less than that.

well, where it meets the face, so that the join here is smooth and well attached. Re-define the dent if necessary as you work, and make sure the muzzle is evenly shaped on both sides.

5. Choose the position for the two eyes, putting a pin into each eye position to better judge whether the eye positions are even, and if they are where you want them to be. I generally prefer them to be sitting just above the join between the muzzle and the rest of the face. Make a dent in each eye position for the eye sockets, using your fine needle, by working repeatedly into the same small area.

6. The ears: These are made as one flat disc shape, and then cut in half, so that you have two half-circles the same size. You need surprisingly little wool for this.

Because the ears are so small and flat, it is a good idea to work them entirely with your finer needle. Pull off a small piece of wool and form a rough circle shape on your foam. On top of the wool place a coin about 2.5 – 3cm diameter (1 – 1$\frac{1}{4}$ins).

Tip: If you make the muzzle big your bear will look big and strong; if you make it little, your bear will look small and cute!

4. Push your needle deeply through the muzzle and into the head, to attach it firmly. You will have to needle for some time to make sure it is firm. Work on the edges of the muzzle as

Make a dent with your felting needle all around the outside of the coin, then remove the coin and fold any stray fibres into the middle of the circle.

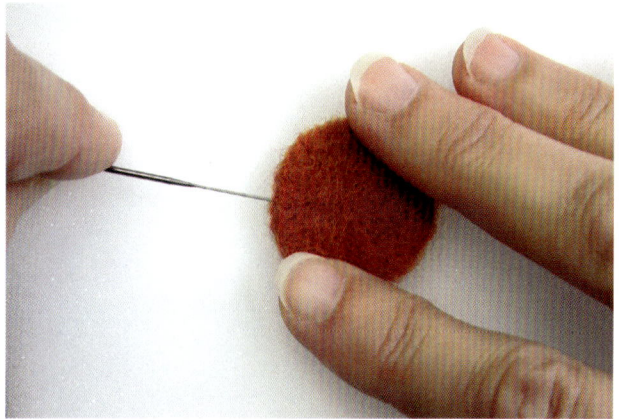

8. Check with the coin to see that the ear is still about the same size. Keep turning the disc over and needling each side. You can also hold your needle flat and push it into the edges of the disc to firm up the wispy edges and control the size. When your disc is holding its shape nicely and feels firm, you are ready to cut it in half and attach each ear to your bear's head.

7. Needle the circle and keep pulling in any wool that strays outside your circular line. Pull the felted disc off the foam, turn it over and felt the other side. Don't push too deeply or you will make more fibres come out underneath your work. You may like to work your needle on an angle sideways so that the fibres don't come out on the other side.

9. Push a pin into the centre top of the bear's head as a guide so that you can place your ears evenly on either side of his head. Needle the top corner of the first ear near the top of the head, about halfway between the front and the back of the head (check with the photos for correct placement). Push the needle down through the ear corner and deeply into the head, repeating quite a few times until it is holding.

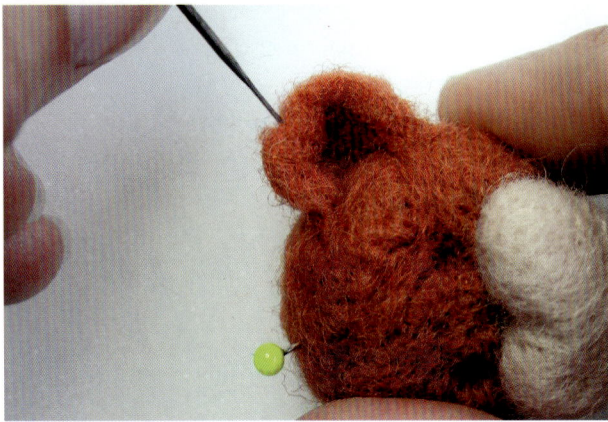

10. Then position the lower corner of the ear, allowing the middle to curve around to the back, and felt that until it is just holding. The ear may look rather too big at the moment, but it will shrink smaller as you felt it. Needle repeatedly right around the back edge of the ear, and also inside the ear, paying particular attention to making sure the corners are firmly felted on. Continue felting for quite some time until you are satisfied that the ear feels very firmly attached, and is about the size that you want it. If it is too big, needle it some more until it shrinks down. To shrink the ear quickly, push your needle from the outside edge straight down into the head several times, then check for size again.

12. If the second ear gets out of line compared to the first, push it back with your fingers and needle to hold it there. You may have to work for a while to get both ears looking the same.

11. Felt the other ear onto the head, making sure that it looks even in size and position with the first ear.

13. **The nose:** This is made from a felted ball of Liquorice wool. You will only need a tiny amount. Shape the wool into a ball on your foam, then needle till firm and round. Place on the muzzle in the dented area and push the needle through the nose and into the muzzle. Continue needling until it is firmly attached, paying particular attention to the edges of the nose, but don't flatten it too much.

Your head will be starting to look like a teddy now, all he needs are his eyes!

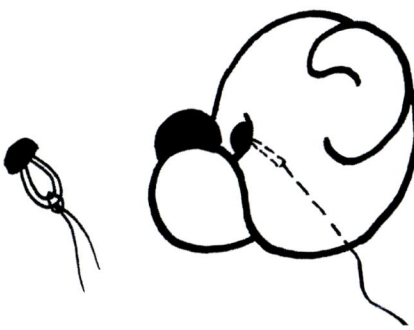

16. The body: The body for your bear is an egg shape, but about twice the size of the head you have made, so use about 23cm (9ins) of wool. Make the body by winding the wool into an oval then felting until it is the size you want the body to be. Shape it into an egg shape by working one end into a slight point.

Give your bear a white tummy by adding a thin layer of Skin wool as indicated in the diagram of basic shapes. You may also like to make a dent to give him a tummy button.

14. The eyes: Use a half hitch knot to attach a 38cm (15ins) length of dental floss folded in half, to the wire loop of one eye. Once the floss is attached squeeze the wire loop closed, using small pliers.

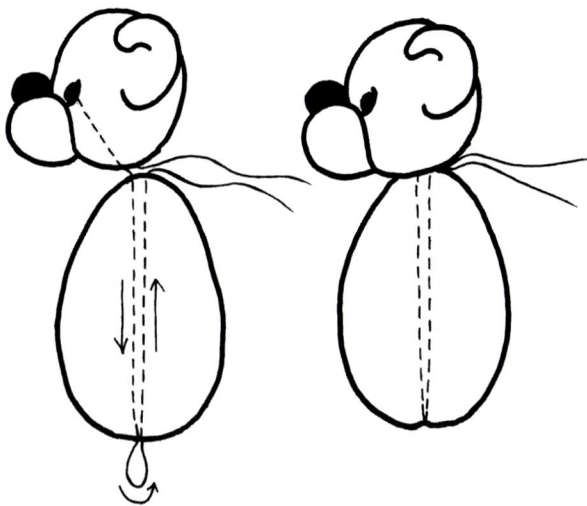

15. Thread both ends of floss from one eye on to a long needle and insert the needle into an eye socket. Bring the needle out at the bottom of the head where the neck will be and leave the thread hanging there. Now do the same for the other eye, coming out about ½cm (¼in) away from the first thread. Pull both threads down to firmly embed the eyes in their sockets, then tie the ends together tightly and leave them at the neck. These ends will be used later to attach the head to the body.

Sew a black thread from the bottom of the nose to the mouth, making an inverted Y shape for the mouth. You may also like to add eyebrows at this stage.

17. Attaching the head to the body: Take one of the double threads that you have left hanging from under the head, and thread it on a long needle (one that is longer than the length of your body). Insert the needle at the neck end of the body, taking it straight down through the body and out at the lower end. Pull the thread all the way through.

19. The legs: Pull off two lengths of sliver about 12.5cm (5ins) long. These will form the two legs. Make the legs by mixing the wool, then wrapping it tightly around a kebab stick and poking it a few times before removing the stick.

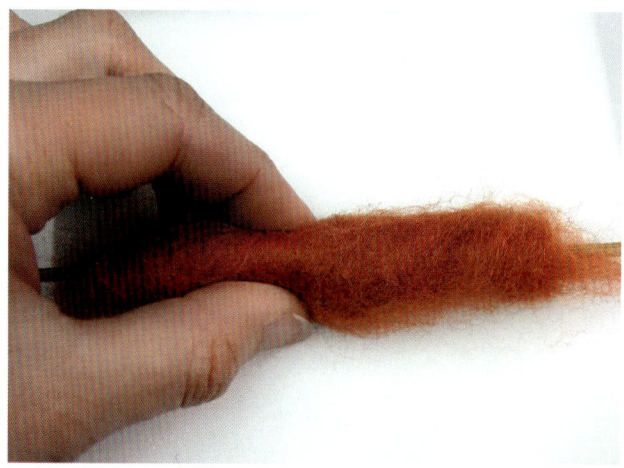

20. The resulting sausage shape needs to be a little bit longer than the length of the leg when finished, plus the length of the foot.

18. Insert your needle back in the same hole as you just came out of and take it back up through the body to exit at the top, just ½cm (¼in) away from where you first inserted the needle. The idea is that you want the thread to disappear back inside the body at the lower end, but to grab some of the felt inside the body to hold on to when you pull tight.

Tie a knot with this thread and the remaining double thread from the other eye. You need to pull this very tight before you tie off the knot, so that the head is set firmly against the body, and not flopping around.

To finish the ends after knotting, take them back through the body with your needle, pull tight, then cut them so that they disappear back into the body. DON'T simply cut them off at the neck edge, or the knot may work itself loose and undo.

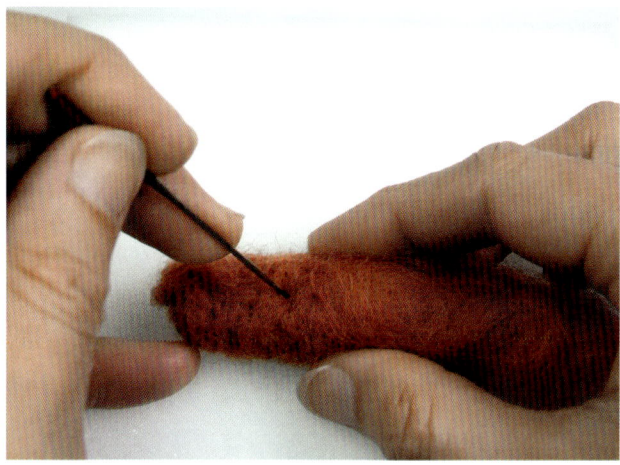

21. Working on the leg part only (and leaving the foot loose till later), firm it up with the felting needle, working the hip area in from the end, to make it a little larger and stronger than the rest of the leg. The hip needs to be very firmly felted for the joint.

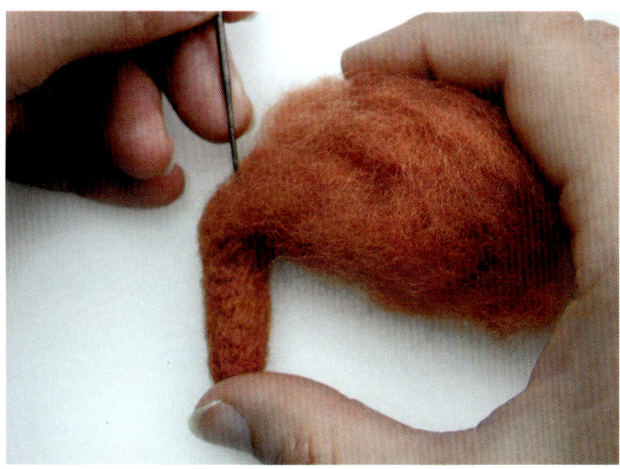

22. When the leg is firm, work the foot. Tease out the wool for the foot a little so that it is loose. To turn the foot, place the leg upside down, bend the loose fibres at right angles to the leg and needle felt from the heel back down into the length of the leg.

23. Now turn your work back up the right way and shape the foot. To ensure that it doesn't flatten out too much, take the wool at the toes and roll it up over itself until you get to the ankle. Needle to hold, then continue working and shaping until the foot is the size you want.

Repeat for the other leg making sure both feet are the same size when finished. I like to make my feet roughly in the shape of a triangle, with the heel being the point, and the toe area being the wider part.

Tip: If all else fails…… If you have tried in vain to get the two feet matching in size, there are two solutions:

First, you could add a little more wool to the **smaller** of the feet and felt this down until the two feet are even.

Or, you can take your scissors to the **larger** of the feet, and cut it down to size. I use small embroidery scissors and trim small amounts off repeatedly until the foot matches the size of the smaller one. Then take a wispy piece of wool and felt this all over the cut edges so that they won't show. You don't want a thick wad that will enlarge the foot again, you are just "skinning" over the cut edges.

Teddybear ... continued

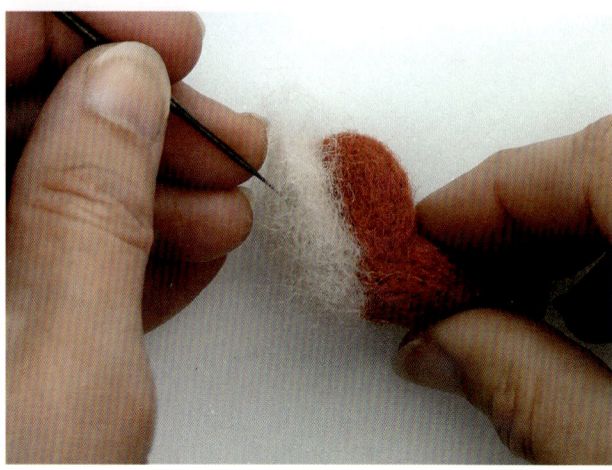

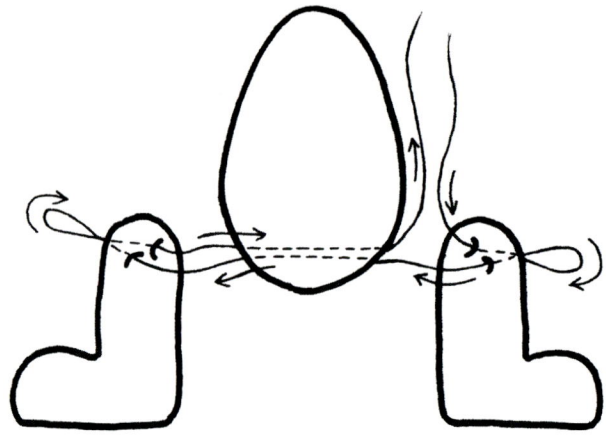

24. Adding pawpads: Make a small flat oval of Skin wool on the bottom of each foot, as you did when attaching the butterfly's spots, making sure the shape and size of the pad is the same on both feet.

25. Jointing the legs: Take a length of dental floss about 38cm (15ins) and thread it on to your long needle, just a single thread. Insert the needle near the top of your first leg, on the *inside* of the leg, and take it out the other side, leaving a length of thread hanging out at the beginning that you can use to tie a knot later. Now go straight back in the same hole as you came out of, and come out beside your first thread, about .25cm ($^{1}/_{8}$in) away. This will allow the dental floss to grab some of the wool in the leg but hide the stitch from the outside. Sit the bear's body on the table, and place the leg against the body so that it is going to be in a nice position when the bear is sitting down. Work out where the needle needs to be inserted in the body to keep that position, and go right through the body and out the other side, keeping the needle level, so that the legs stay the same height.

Take a stitch through the other leg, from the *inside* to the *outside*, and then back in the same hole and out .25cm ($^{1}/_{8}$in) away.

Now take the needle back through the body and come out close to where it went in. Tie a knot using the thread that is hanging out of the first leg and the thread from the body, pulling the legs in very tightly so that they fit snugly, and are not floppy. Bury the ends back in the body.

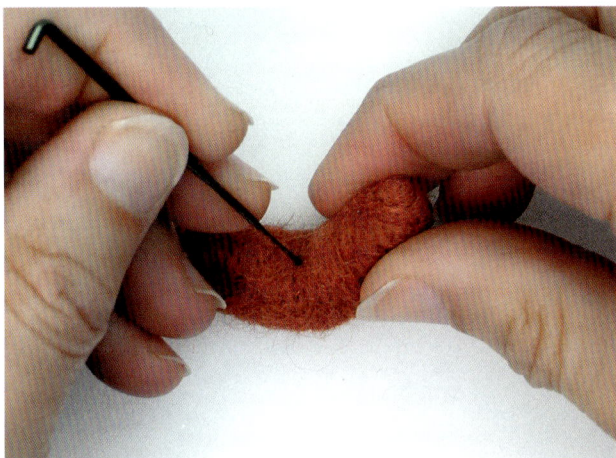

26. The arms: Make two cylinder shapes for the arms, smaller than the legs, using a kebab stick again. Felt the arm down, paying attention to both ends, as the paws and the shoulders need to be firm. When it is about half-felted, make a bend for the elbow, about halfway along the arm, by pressing your thumbnail where you want the bend to be, and working repeatedly into the dent. Make the other arm the same and attach pawpads as for the foot, if desired. The elbow bends don't have to be the same for each arm. You can have one arm loosely bent and the other very tightly bent so that he can bring his arm up to his mouth, as our teddy is doing.

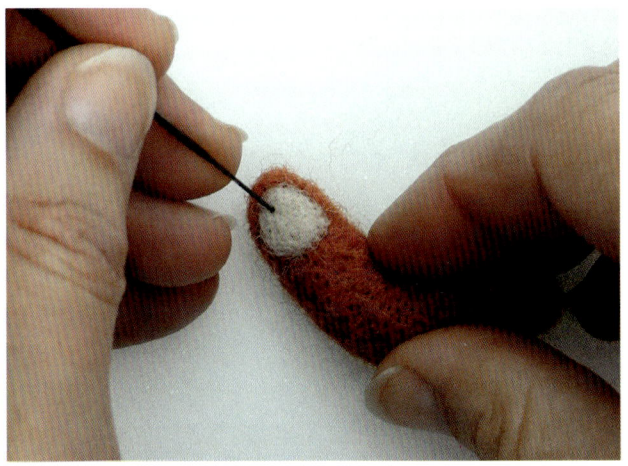

27. Jointing the arms: Join the two arms on to the body in the same way as you did the legs, but this time you need to decide how far down from the head that you want to place the arms. If they are very high up, your teddy will look like he is shrugging his shoulders; if you put them a bit lower down he will look more relaxed. It really depends on what look you prefer. To try the positions out, put a pin through the arm at the shoulder and pin it to the body. That will give you an idea of what he will look like.

And that's it; your teddy is now complete. I am sure you will be delighted with him!

Vest
Project 4

This men's sleeveless vest will be perfect for keeping warm in the great outdoors. You can vary the motif according to the interests of the person wearing it, but this leaping trout will appeal to many keen fishermen. I am sure you will agree it creates a very individual-looking vest. You could decorate clothing for hunting, golfing, etc. Flower motifs or animals would look wonderful, too.

Materials:
Merino wool sliver Beansprout, Green Tea, Strawberry Shortcake, Chocolate, Liquorice, White, Lagoon, Spearmint – small pieces of each colour*
Corriedale wool sliver Cookie – small piece*
Polar fleece vest
Water soluble stabiliser
Felting needle 38S
*Total amount of all the wool is about 5gm ($1/8$oz)

Finished size: 12.3cm ($4^3/_4$ins) – trout only – not including water

1. Begin by tracing the trout pattern onto the stabiliser. Lay the vest over a piece of foam and pin the stabiliser pattern in place. Needle a mix of Beansprout and Chocolate wool over the tail and three fins, allowing it to flow over the body of the fish. Later layers will cover the rough edges but the outside edges of the fins should be neatly finished.

Vest ... continued

2. Add small pieces of wool, one at a time, to help keep control over how the wool is shaped. Make the fin under the belly a darker brown, as it is coming from the other side of his body and is in shadow.

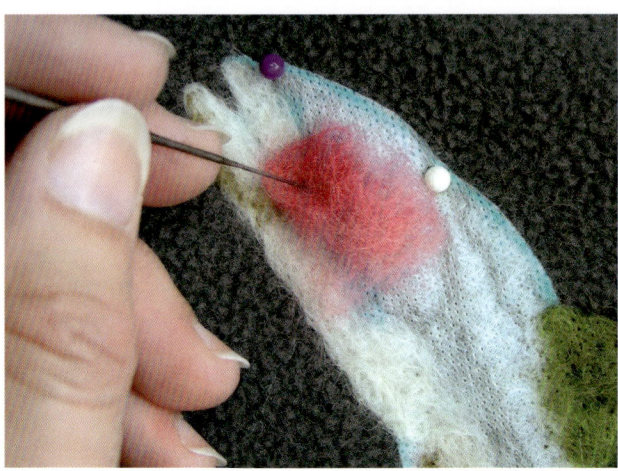

4. Small pieces of Cookie wool, needled thinly under the mouth and between the tail and the middle fins, will help shade these areas.

3. Add White wool to the underbelly and lower face, feathering it out where it will meet the wool from the body.

5. The warm stripe in the middle can be done with Strawberry Shortcake wool, feathered out softly onto the underbelly.

Tip: If you find that you are getting a harsh line where two colours meet, take a large sewing needle, tease out the fibres until the line disappears, then continue needle felting. You could also use your scissors to cut the edge fibres in some places before teasing out.

6. Lay a band of mixed Green Tea and Chocolate wool over the top of the fish's back, feathering it down over the pink central band so there is a soft progression from one colour to the next. We don't want a harsh line here, so tease out the edges of the green mix as you felt it over the pink.

7. Add some of this mixture behind the gills to define the shape, and over the top of the face. Vary the width of the dark green so that where it joins the pink doesn't look like a straight line. This will add more visual interest. I have added a dark brown stripe right at the edge of the fish, but this is not really necessary, unless your vest is dark and there is not much contrast between the fish and the fabric.

8. Pull out some thin strands of dark wool and needle them in place on the tail and fins.

9. Make a small pale circle for the eye, and then needle a Liquorice wool pupil in the centre. Add some very thin lines to outline the gills.

10. Needle the second fin under the belly and the fin behind the gills in the same colours as the others, adding thin strands of wool on top as before.

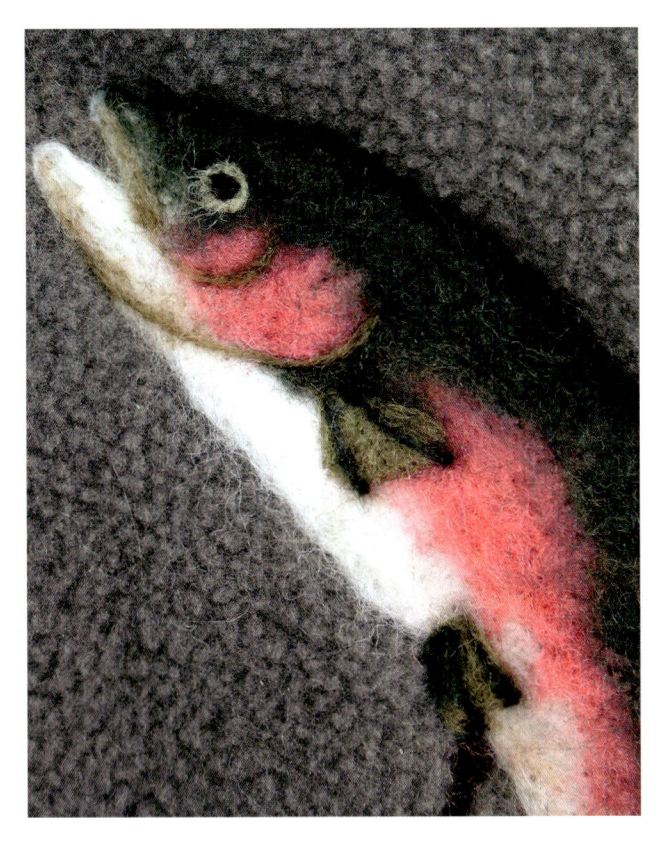

11. Now your fish is finished! All that is needed is the splashing water. You don't have to use a pattern for this part, just make it freestyle. Start with a layer of White wool and needle as indicated in the picture, fanning the wool out to look like water splashing. Add some blue and turquoise wool in the centre of the splash, under the tail area, to give depth.

And there you have your water. So very simple! Go over your motif now with your needle punch tool, making sure that the wool is firmly felted down all over the pattern. Pull the vest off the foam and check the underside of the work. You may like to needle some of the fibres slantwise to tidy the back, although it doesn't really matter. If there is any stabiliser showing around the edges of the fish, use a tiny paintbrush to daub it with warm water and it will disappear. Remember to treat the vest as you would a woollen garment when washing.

Danish pastry

Project 5

Felted food is such fun to make and leave on a plate on your coffee table. You may find your guests look a little confused when they see it, wondering if it is real or not!

You will need:
Merino wool sliver Scarlet 12gm ($3/8$oz), White 1gm ($1/32$oz), Indigo 2gm ($1/16$oz), Beansprout small piece
Corriedale wool sliver Honey 12gm ($3/8$oz) and small pieces of Toffee, Butterscotch and Cookie
Felting needles 38S, 40T

Finished size: 10.5cm ($4\frac{1}{4}$ins) diameter

I have made this pastry softly felted (unlike the teddybear, which is firmly felted), as I think the softness reflects the bread-like quality of the pastry.

1. The pastry base: Take an 18cm (7ins) length of Honey wool, curl it into a flat circle, then felt it down lightly, using a 38S needle.

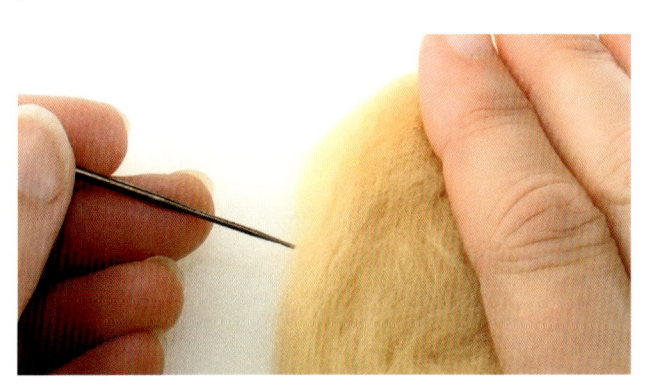

2. Pull the wool off the foam and turn over, working on the reverse side as well. Push your needle into the side of the circle to firm up the edge, turning and repeating until you have a round disc about 1cm ($1/2$in) thick and 8.5cm ($3 1/2$ins) across. This is the base of the pastry.

3. Next we will add the twisted pastry edge. Use a length of Honey wool about 40cm ($15 3/4$ins) long. Split it evenly in two, lengthwise, then work each piece into a thin, long sausage shape, softly felted, and leaving the ends loose and wispy.

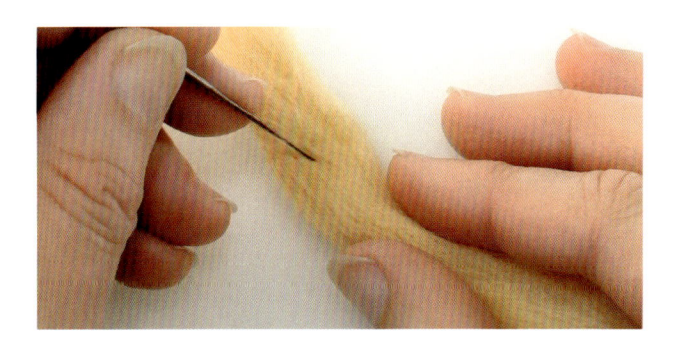

4. Twist the two sausage shapes around each other, and needle the ends onto the base, blending them in so they are level with the base wool.

5. Arrange several twists around the outside edge of the base and carefully needle them to attach, trying not to lose too much of the twisted effect. Work into the bottom edges of the twist, both outside and inside the circle, and also in the line between the two twisted pieces. When these twists are attached, arrange several more and attach them, continuing to work right around the base until you get back to the beginning.

6. Finish off the inner rope by needling it to the inside edge of the first twist, cutting it short if necessary.

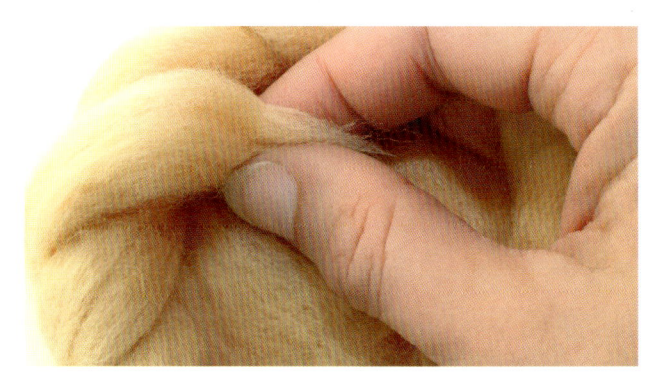

7. Then fold over the remaining rope to cover these cut ends and once again needle against the inside edge of the first twist.

You should have an almost invisible join.

8. These inner edges will be covered by the filling, so don't have to be perfect. Turn the work over and needle from the base back up into the twists, to make a strong join.

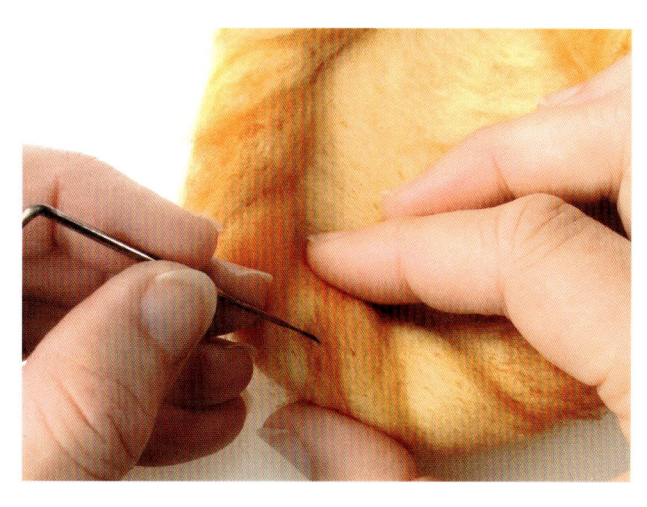

10. When the Butterscotch has been felted down, add another thin layer, this time of Toffee, making the fibres only about 2.5cm (1in) long, and placing them on top where the oven will have baked it darker than on the sides. Once again, make the layer uneven, and not as much as the Butterscotch colour.

9. To give your pastry the illusion of being baked golden brown, pull off some thin wisps of Butterscotch wool as shown, about 3cm (1 1/2 ins) long. Tease them out till they are very thin, and lay them on the twisted ropes, making sure the fibres are lying in the same direction as the twists. Needle lightly to hold in place, and repeat all over the twisted edge. These wisps do not need to be evenly placed and you should allow a lot of the Honey to still show through.

11. Now fill the pastry with cream. Add a layer of White wool to the centre, needling it just enough to hold it in place, while leaving it with the fluffy look of whipped cream.

Danish pastry ... continued

12. The strawberries: Make the three strawberries with 15cm (6ins) of Scarlet wool each, beginning with a short cylinder. Shape it with a rounded point on one end, wide and flatter at the other.

13. If the surface of the berry is a little bit rough, it doesn't matter as the bumps and hollows will indicate where the strawberry seeds would be. Felt the strawberries a little firmer than the pastry.

14. Place the three berries evenly on the cream, and felt them down, working deeply into the base of the pastry.

15. Once attached, turn the pastry over and needle back up through the base and into each berry. You could also needle repeatedly through the lower part of one berry into the next one, to join them all together.

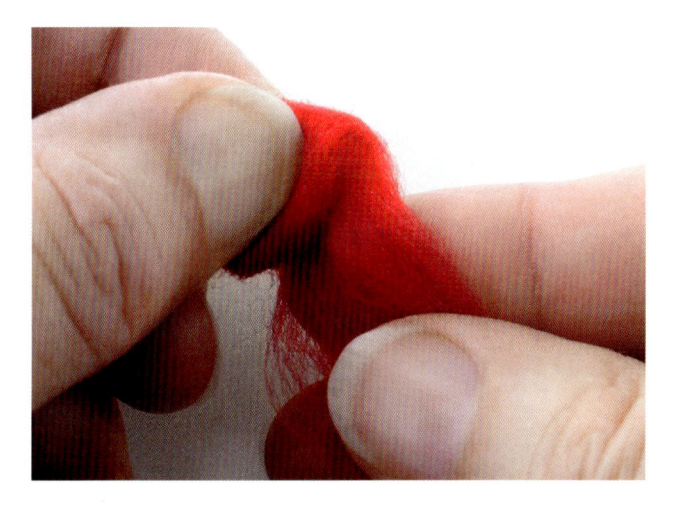

16. The remaining berries: Make the redcurrants by pulling off a length of Scarlet wool 10cm (4ins) long, and dividing it into four pieces. Fold over the end of one piece, holding it tightly in your fingers, then fold it again on a slight angle. Continue in this way, folding on opposite angles, until you have tightly folded the complete length.

18. Needle a small wisp of Beansprout wool into the berry, leaving the wool sticking out a little way, like a tiny leaf. Make four berries the same.

17. Needle to hold, then work into a small round ball. You may like to change to a 40T needle for these berries, as they are so small, although the 38S will still achieve the results you want.

Danish pastry ... continued

19. Pull off a thin piece of Beansprout for the stem, about 11cm (4½ins) long, fold in half and twist with your fingers, then lay it down on the foam and felt it, rolling and twisting repeatedly to keep the stem narrow and round, not flattened out.

20. To make the three shorter stems, take a wisp of wool about 3.5cm (1½ins) long and place on top of one of the berries, on the opposite side to the green already inserted. Needle repeatedly into the middle of the green wool so that it is pushed into the berry and holding firmly.

21. Now fold the two halves of this stem together and needle as you did the longer stem. Repeat until you have three berries with short stems.

22. You will have an end on the large stem that is wispy. Use these fibres to push deeply into the last berry to attach it to the stem. Lay one of the short stems with berry onto the larger one, just beneath the first berry, and felt on firmly. Add another stem on the other side, then the final berry at the bottom, felting all the stems firmly together.

23. Make the blueberries with Indigo wool, using the same method as above, but the berries should be slightly larger. Needle a wisp of Cookie wool into the berry in a tiny circle, but this time work until it is level with the surface of the berry.

24. Make a half strawberry in a similar way to how you made the main ones, but keep one side flat. Add a wisp of White wool to the flat side, feathering it out at the edges and making the white denser towards the middle. Needle a thin strip of red wool in the centre.

For the strawberry leaves, take a tiny piece of Beansprout wool and felt it into a flat oval shape, pointed at each end. Firm up the edges of the leaves by holding between your thumb and forefinger and carefully jiggle the needle in and out, working right around the edges. You will find this method works wonders at defining and firming up the edges. The idea is to have the wool held way back between your fingers so that the tip of the needle never has to come out from between your fingers as you work, therefore it can't hurt you. Make a 'waist' in the leaves by denting in the middle on both sides, then place over the top of the strawberry and felt the middle part deeply into the berry to attach.

Place your delightful Danish Pastry on a plate on your coffee table, and enjoy! You could make a variety of cakes and pastries, or even some larger fruit.

Tote bag

Project 6

This bag has a brightly coloured needle felted flap on a black background, reminiscent of a peacock feather, making it quite a striking feature. It also has a bright purple lining. By choosing different colours you could make a softer-looking bag (eg. pinks and lilacs).

You will need:
Merino wool sliver Lagoon 1gm ($^1/_{32}$oz),
Liquorice 4gm ($^1/_8$oz)
Corriedale wool sliver Lemon 4gm ($^1/_8$oz),
Green 6gm ($^1/_4$oz), Purple 2gm ($^1/_{16}$oz)
Black fabric for bag
Purple fabric for lining
Cord for closure
Thin batting
Water soluble stabiliser
Felting needle 38S

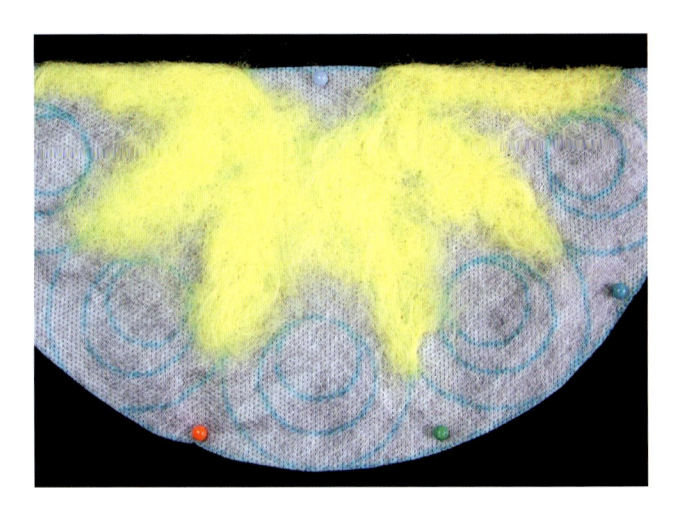

2. Needle felt the flap before cutting out the fabric. Cut a piece of black fabric slightly larger than needed for the back and flap pattern. Trace the pattern for the bag flap onto the stabiliser and pin it through your backing fabric onto a foam block. When using stabiliser on dark fabric, remember that once it has been dissolved away you will be left with the dark colour behind it, so make sure your wool fibres are felted on thickly enough so that the black fabric won't show through when the white stabiliser is washed away.

Begin filling in the pattern using a 38S needle. Start with the Lemon wool and allow it to flow past the lines into the next colour section. The colours in the later layers will cover the rough edges of the Lemon to make a sharp line. Don't worry if your work looks a bit messy at this stage, although you will need to make the outside edges of the design neat and well defined, as these will show on the finished bag.

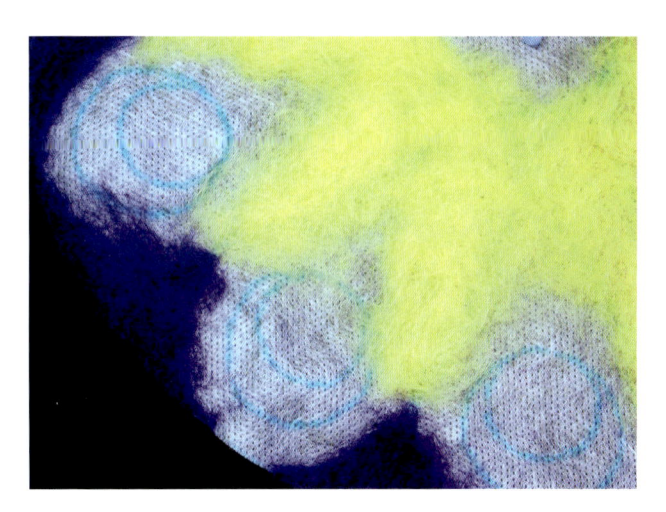

Finished size: 24cm (9$^1/_2$ins) wide at base

1. Enlarge the pattern pieces (on page 92) to the size you require. This bag was made from the pattern enlarged to an A3 size or 29.5 x 42cm (11$^1/_2$ins x 16$^1/_2$ins) w x h sheet of paper. Please note that the pattern does not have seam allowances, as these will alter depending on how much you enlarge the pattern, so add these after enlarging.

3. Needle the Purple on the outer edge next, overlapping it slightly again, so that the Green of the peacock feathers can be needled later over the top to define the edges.

Tote bag ... continued

4. Once these under-layers are felted on you may no longer be able to see the design clearly, so simply draw the next pattern piece (e.g. the peacock feather) on some more stabiliser, cut out and pin it over the top of your work. You can then felt on top of this and see clearly where the lines need to go.

5. To help position each new feather correctly, draw the complete design onto tracing paper and hold this over the top of your work. You will be able to see through this to position the new stabiliser feather. Remove the tracing paper and pin the feather in position. Do this for each of the peacock feathers, one at a time, and repeat for any other parts of the design which have been covered by previous layers of wool. You can have several layers of stabiliser, one on top of the other, and it won't make any difference, as long as the wool is felted firmly through it.

6. When shaping the end of the feathers, twist the wool in your fingers until it forms a point, then lay it down over the pattern piece and felt on.

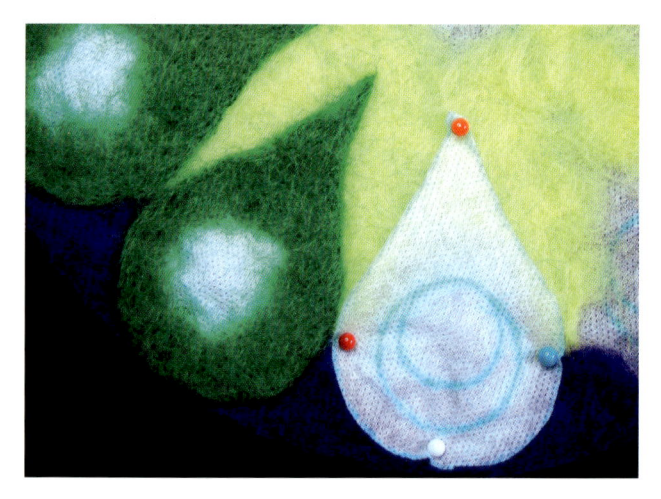

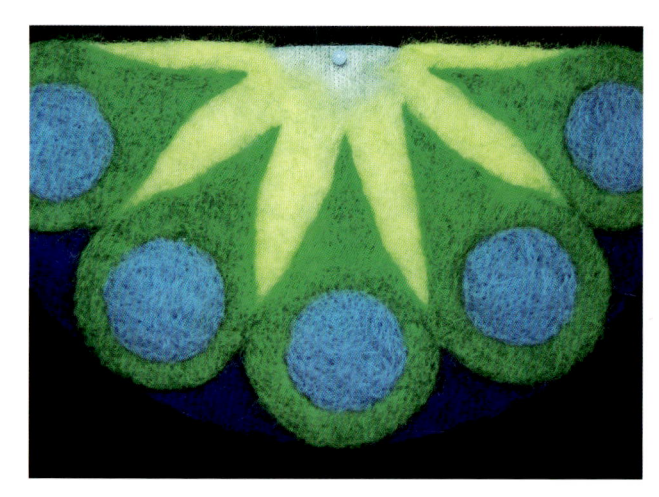

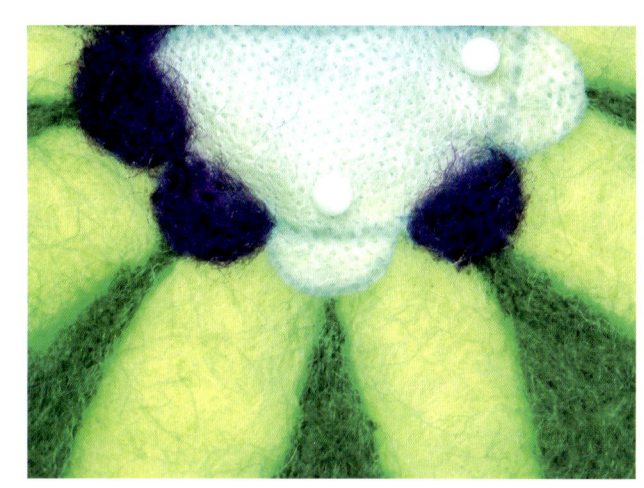

7. Build up the other colours, making sure you achieve sharp lines where the colours change. Add more wool wherever you feel that a shape is too small or thin or does not meet where it should.

8. Remove your work from the foam. It should not be necessary to wash out the stabiliser if it is completely covered with your felting, but you can so at this point if you wish. Trim any stray fibres from the felt and decorate with beads if desired.

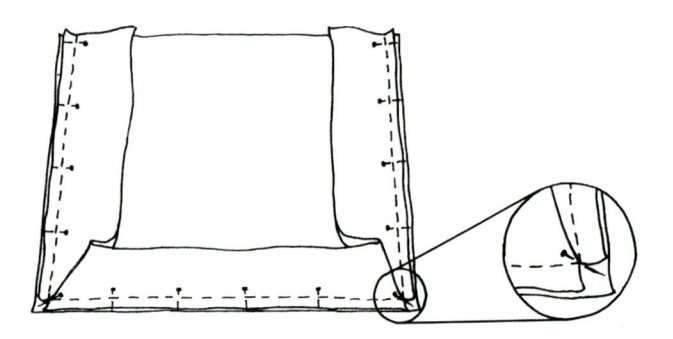

9. Cut the flap and bag back according to the pattern, leaving a seam allowance around the edge of the needle felting, which will be turned under when the lining is stitched on. Cut out all other pattern pieces. Pin the gusset to the front of the bag, clip the corners, then stitch.

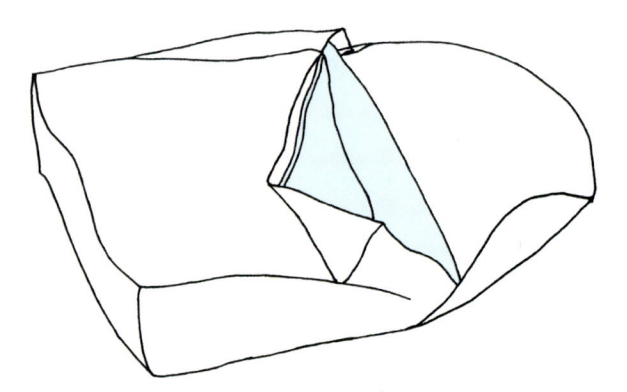

11. Cut batting (you don't need to allow seams on this piece), and insert inside the bag. Trim the batting so that the top edges are sitting just below where the finished seam line will be, and whip stitch in place across the top edges, making stitches invisible on the outside of the bag.

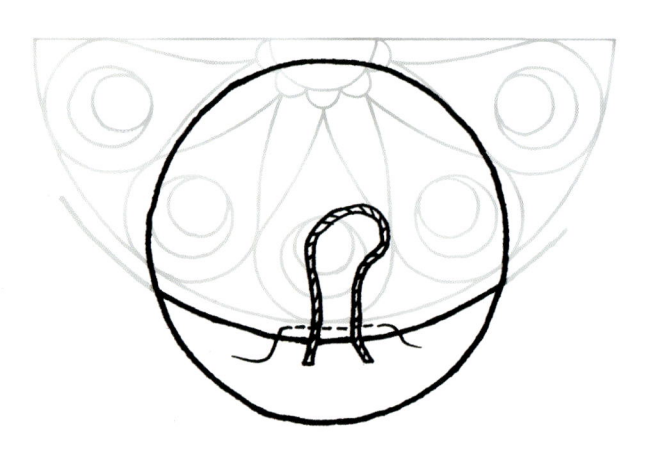

10. Pin the mid-point of the bag back to the mid-point of the gusset. Then pin the rest of the gusset to the back, clipping corners, and stitch. Begin and end your stitching a seam-width away from each end of the gusset. Turn right side out.

12. Stitch a loop of cord to the centre of the needlefelted flap, as shown.

13. Cut and stitch the lining using the same pattern pieces and instructions as for the main bag, but the lining flap is not needle felted.

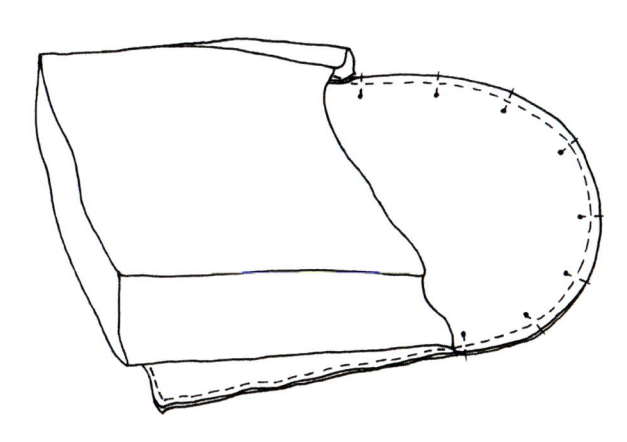

14. With right sides together, pin and stitch the needle felted flap to the lining flap, using a zipper foot or similar, to allow you to stitch as close as possible to the edge of the felt.

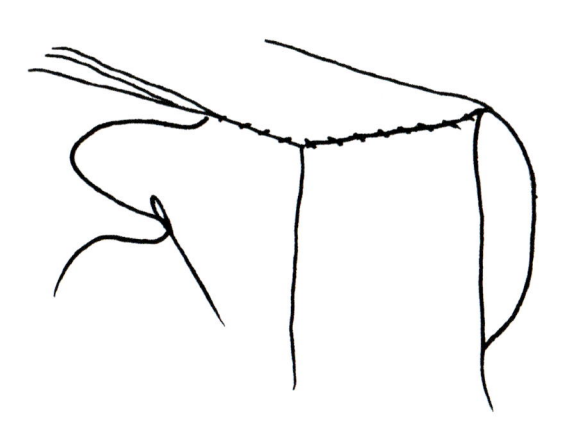

15. Stop sewing when you reach the gusset seam allowance at the sides. Clip the curves and turn, tucking the lining inside the bag. Fold in the seam allowances around the top and slip stitch together.

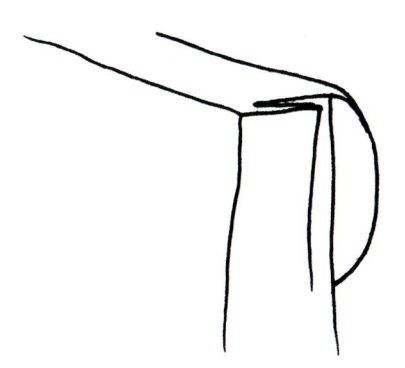

16. Fold the strap together lengthwise and stitch. Turn right side out and press. Make a tuck in each side of the bag at the top of the gusset, so that it is the same width as the strap. Stitch to hold.

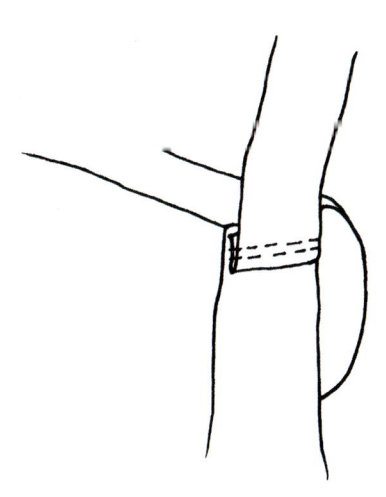

17. Stitch the strap in place on top of the tuck, turning under the raw edges as you do so.

18. Make a small, firm needle felted ball and attach to the front of the bag, using the corded loop to close. You may like to cover this ball with beads matching the colours of the needle felted flap, or make it from multi-coloured wools to match the felting. Add more beads, braids or tassels to the design and your bag is finished!

Iris blooms
Project 7

These irises are so delicate and fine looking, but very easy to make. They are needle felted onto stabiliser with wire added for shaping. The petals are dipped in water when finished to dissolve the backing, and then joined to the stem. And there you have it – a very realistic needle felted iris. You can use the techniques here to make many different flower shapes, and also leaves to complement the flowers.

You will need:
Merino wool sliver Cheesecake 1gm ($1/32$oz),
White 4gm ($1/8$oz), Beansprout 12gm ($3/8$oz)
Corriedale wool sliver Lavender 8gm ($1/4$oz),
Lime 2gm ($1/16$oz)
Water soluble stabiliser
Craft Wire 0.45mm (28 gauge) 0.9mm wire (24 gauge)
Felting needle 38S

Finished size: Life size approx. 30cm (12ins) tall

1. Trace the iris petal patterns onto the stabiliser. You will need three upper petals and three lower petals per flower. We are going to use VERY thin layers of wool in this flower, to keep it looking light and delicate. You will find it best to use a fine needle (38S), so that you don't have too many wispy bits coming out the back. A needle punch tool with fine needles would be ideal, as it would speed up the needle felting process.

2. Make the three upright petals first. Cut three upper petal pattern pieces in stabiliser. Pin one of these to the foam. Lay small thin pieces of Lavender wool all over the pattern, allowing a small amount to flow past the edges of the pattern.

3. You should be able to almost see through this layer. Change the colour of the wool as you get closer to the stem, making the lower part of the petal white.

4. Needle felt this layer lightly, using a multi-needle tool if you have one. Don't felt over the edges at this stage. Take the pins out as soon as the wool has attached the stabiliser to the foam. Use the dent-and-fold method to define the outer edge of the petal.

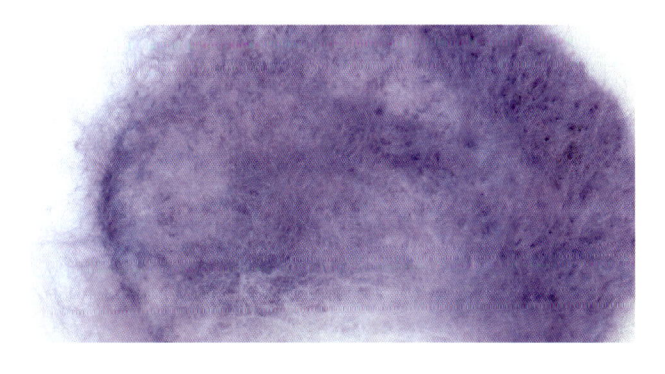

Iris blooms ... continued

5. If you notice any very thin patches at this stage, simply place a small amount of wool over the area and needle it in place. Pull the petal off the foam, and clean any remaining wool out of the foam. This will stop any more wispy bits being attached to the petal as you continue to work.

7. Make a thin Lavender sausage by rolling it in your fingers and then needling lightly. Add some white wool to the lower end, so that the sausage is the same length as the petal when finished.

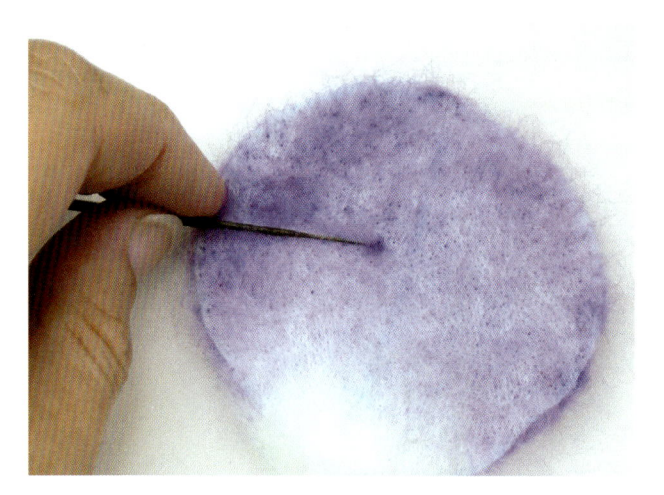

6. Turn the petal over and needle from the back to felt in any wisps of wool, laying your needle sideways as much as possible to prevent making more wisps on the other side. Tidy up the outside edges again.

8. Cut a piece of fine wire about 15 – 20cm (6 – 7ins) and turn over one end. Lay this on top of the petal, starting just below the top edge, and extending down past the base of the petal. We will use the extra length later to join the petals together.

9. Place the wool sausage over the wire, starting at the tip of the petal where the wire is rounded over. Make sure you needle around the tip of the wire firmly to hold it in place, then needle down each side of the sausage, covering the wire as you go.

10. Feather the edges of this ridge so that they blend in to the rest of the petal, but don't flatten the sausage totally as we need it to appear as a ridge down the centre of the petal. Be careful not to accidentally pull out the wire at this stage.

Tip: To feather a join that you don't want to show, snip some of the edge fibres where they form a line, spacing the snips about 1cm (1/2in) apart. Then take a pin or sewing needle and tease out the cut edges. Needle felt these wispy fibres down to blend them in to the background.

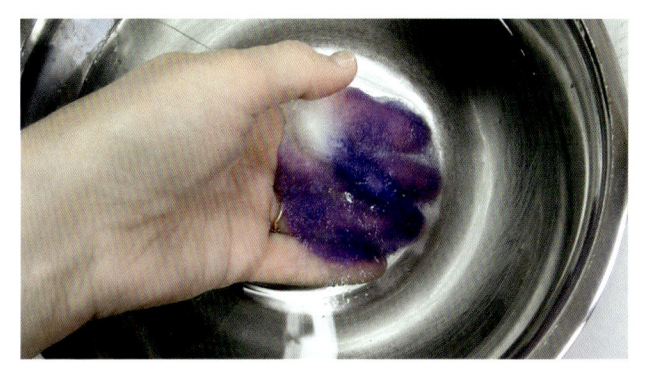

11. Make three petals the same, and then rinse them in warm water to dissolve the stabiliser (support each petal on your fingers as you rinse it, because it is very thin).

12. You will need to squeeze the wool gently between your fingers to make sure that all the stabiliser is rinsed out. While wet, the petal will appear quite transparent, but this will disappear once it is dry. Pat the petals between two towels and leave till they are completely dry. If you find that the central ridge has flattened out too much after rinsing, pinch it back up with your fingers while it is still damp. Once the petals are dry, curve them as in the pictures, with the wired ridge on the outside.

13. The lower petals are made in a similar way. Change from Lavender to White wool where it is indicated on the pattern. Add the central wire covered by a sausage shape of Lavender with White at the base, although this sausage does not need to be raised as much as on the upper petals. Once the petal has been rinsed and dried, add the yellow stamens by lightly needling some Cheesecake wool over the lower part of the petal. Leave this wool looking light and fluffy so that it sits up above the petal surface.

15. Make three lower petals the same. Trim any wispy fibres from the petals before joining them. To join these six petals into a flower, take one of the lower petals, place an upper petal beside it, with the ridge facing outwards, add another lower petal, etc.

14. To make this petal curve downwards, bend the wire stem down, then needle felt sideways on each side close to where the White changes to the Lilac. By holding your needle almost flat against the felt, and working it along sideways, it will pull the felt together in that area, almost like taking a small tuck or dart. You will need to hold the felt between your fingers, so slide the needle SLOWLY in and out through the felt that is between your fingers. You don't want to prick yourself.

16. Repeat till you have three upper petals and three lower petals positioned evenly, as in the picture.

17. Take another length of wire and wrap it around all the wire stems to hold them, leaving a long end hanging down which will form the flower stem. Check that the petals are still in the correct position, and bend them back into place if necessary. At this stage don't bend them to their final display position, as it will be easier to work on the stem with all the petals facing upwards.

18. Use some of the coarse wire for the stem. Cut this wire twice as long as you want the final stem to be, and once one end is wrapped around at the top just beneath the flower, fold it in half at the lower end and wrap the wire around itself to make the stem thicker and also give something for the wool to attach itself around.

19. You may like to add an iris bud or two partway down the stem. To make a bud, wrap a sausage shape of Lime wool the size of the finished bud around a piece of thin wire, remembering to loop the top end of the wire. Make the top of the bud pointed. Now using the pattern for the upper iris petal, make one petal the same colour as the iris, but when you get halfway down change to white wool and leave the lower ends wispy and unformed. Wash the stabiliser off and when dry, wrap the petal around the green bud and felt in place, as in the picture, making sure you keep the upper end pointed. When wrapping the bud around the wire stem, remember that the petals of the flower above it will be bending down, so make sure your bud is positioned low enough to still show.

20. Wrap some Lime wool around the base of the iris to cover the bare wires and felt in place, being careful not to break your needle on the wires underneath. Work a little of this wool back up into the base of the flower to keep it attached there. Change to Beansprout wool as you get further down from the flower (about 3cm or 1^1/$_2$ins), then continue to wrap and felt until the stem is covered and is the thickness required.

21. Because the stem is thin and contains wire, you may find it easier to hold the needle nearly flat against the stem and felt sideways along the length, instead of the normal straight up and down motion. Needle the stem until it is smooth and even. Now adjust your petals so that the ones with the yellow stamens hang down and the three upper petals cluster together above, using the centre wires to bend them where needed.

Now your iris is finished! You may like to make a whole vase full of irises. Just think of all the beautiful colours that irises come in, what a wonderful vase of flowers you could make!

French street scene
Project 8

This typical scene of a street in France is ideal for needle felting work, as the tall buildings are basically block-shaped, with window and door details added. The shadows can be laid over the top of the wool colours afterwards, to give the buildings a 3-dimensional feel, and the contrast of light against dark gives a good focal point in the centre of the picture. The finer details can be enhanced with a little embroidery. You will learn a little about shading here, blending one colour into the next, and also mixing colours. The picture can be stretched and framed when finished; a black mat around it will set the scene off dramatically.

Some of the colours below have been blended together by hand to get the tone needed.

You will need:
Merino wool sliver Honey 12gm ($3/8$oz),
Lagoon 2gm ($1/16$oz), Liquorice 2gm ($1/16$oz),
Chocolate 6gm ($1/4$oz), Scarlet 6gm ($1/4$oz)
Corriedale wool sliver Bubblegum 6gm ($1/4$oz),
White 10gm ($3/8$oz), Lavender 4gm ($1/8$oz), Grey 12gm ($3/8$oz), Nutmeg 12gm ($3/8$oz), Skin 6gm ($1/4$oz),
Peach 10gm ($3/8$oz)
Water soluble stabiliser
Black felted fabric for backing
Embroidery cottons
Felting needle 38S

Finished size: 29.5cm ($11^1/_2$ins) high

This picture is A4 size or 21 x 29.5cm ($8^1/_4$ x $11^1/_2$ins) w x h, although you can make it larger if you wish. I have worked the entire project using a fine needle (38S). Cut the black felt backing with at least 10cm (4ins) extending beyond the pattern on all sides. This will give you allowance for a border around the edge, as well as stretching the picture later for framing. Trace the pattern onto your stabiliser and pin it to the black felt, with a large piece of foam behind all this to support it while you work.

1. Sky: We will work from the background towards the foreground, starting with the sky. This is shaded from mid-blue down to cream as it approaches the rooftops. For my flat felted projects I cut or break up the fibres for mixing to a length of 2.5cm – 5cm (1 – 2ins). This helps prevent the unwanted effect of having long lines of fibre where I don't want them. It also makes it easier when I am blending two colours together.

French street scene ... continued

2. Place White wool loosely at the base of the sky and needle along the lines of the rooftops. The fibres need to be laid on thickly enough so that the stabiliser is completely covered. Work the White up the sky about two-thirds of the way, then change to Bubblegum over the rest of the sky, feathering where they join.

4. **Central building:** Work the dark windows first with a mixture of Liquorice and White wool to make a dark grey. The windows are long and thin, so roll some short thin sausage shapes, then fill in the windows.

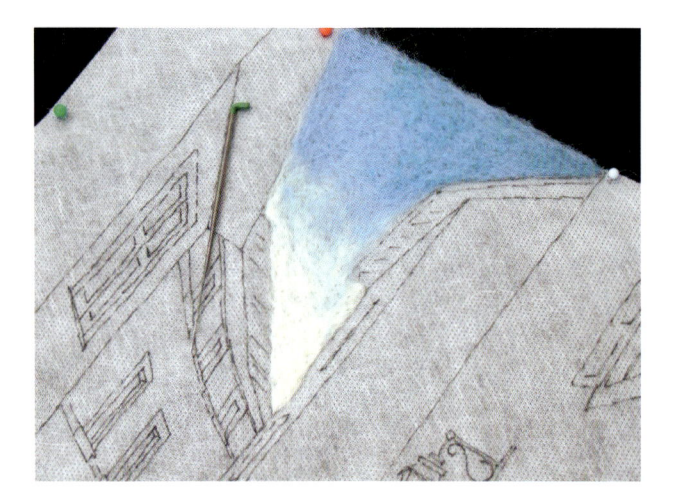

3. You may like to mix a little Lagoon wool into the very top part of the sky, but don't make it too dark, just a subtle hint. Then felt the whole sky down thoroughly. A needle punch tool is excellent for this.

5. Fill in the walls with a pale mix of White and Lavender, keeping it very pale around where the people will go.

6. Make three thin stripes below the windows and roof, and then add White surrounds to the windows and door. Use Chocolate underneath the roof. You can embroider a few lines afterwards to indicate the direction of the rafters or use wool if preferred. The two streetlights on this building will be embroidered later.

7. **Middle right building:** This building is a soft pinkish-apricot, but the side facing the sun is very pale, almost cream. Work the pale side first using Skin wool, down to the top of the awning, then add three thin dark shapes down this wall to suggest windows, although the angle is such that you can't see much detail on them.

The roof is done in grey and brown, and the rafters suggested with slightly darker colour mixes.

Needle the door at the top of the steps using a rough mixture of browns to suggest panelling. This colour can also be used to suggest a door underneath the steps.

8. Use a mixture of Skin and Peach for the rest of the building, bringing the colour down past the side of the steps. The steps can be made in pale grey colours, roughly mixed for texture. Once you have the base colour on, add thin sausages of Honey/White mix to suggest where the brilliant sun is reflecting off the top of each step.

10. The dark and lighter shading can be achieved simply by varying the thickness of the layer of wool, but make sure it is still thin enough to allow the original colour to shine through.

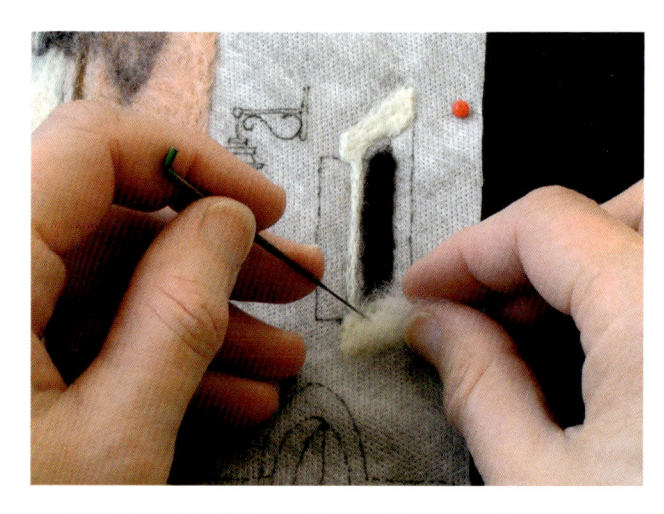

9. Add the roof shadow to the top of the building by using a very thin, wispy layer of Chocolate over the top of the wall colour, shading to deeper brown under the eaves of the roof, and in the doorway. Add pale grey edging to the roof.

11. **Right hand building:** This building is soft Honey, with Bubblegum shutters, windows and door. Work the window and door surrounds with White.

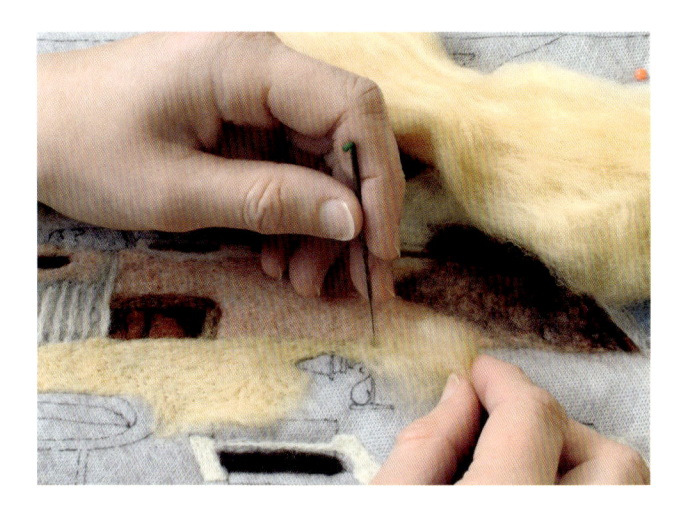

12. Remember to make the shadows around the shutters very dark brown/grey, to indicate the strength of the sun. Make the hanging streetlight using a triangle of White wool and a smaller triangle of Liquorice wool above it, no detail, as this will be embroidered later.

French street scene ... continued

13. Left hand building: This building is filled in with Peach wool, and the darker shutters outlined in Chocolate. Use the same greyish mix as in the steps for the doorway surround. The rafters under the roof can be defined with Chocolate.

14. Far left wall: Work this in Nutmeg wool, to make it a little darker than the building beside it. There should be little or no detail on this wall so that it doesn't draw the eye.

15. Street surface: Begin to lay down the surface of the street around the two figures, making it a pale mixture of natural coloured wools, and allowing the mix to get darker as you work towards the bottom of the picture.

16. Final details: Work the shadowed area under the awning in Chocolate, with Bubblegum for the step. For the three plants, felt the containers first, then mix two different greens roughly and felt the foliage.

17. The two figures are felted using bright colours, so that you have a good contrast between them and their surroundings. There doesn't have to be a lot of detail in these figures, just the general shape.

18. Add the red awning, and use a rough mixture of darker greys for the large foreground step, with a few dark lines to indicate the individual stones.

19. **Foreground shadows:** Use thin wisps of wool to add shadows running across the street, starting from the left and climbing up across the right front building, making the shadows darker as you get closer to the bottom of the picture. This will allow the eye to be led in to the centre of the picture where the figures are standing.

20. **Finishing touches:** Go over the whole picture with your needle punch tool to make sure everything is thoroughly felted, then use a paint brush dipped in warm water to dissolve any edges of stabiliser that are still showing. Remove the picture from the foam, peeling it off carefully.

Use embroidery for the details on the right hand street light, the lights on the rear wall and the stair rail. Define the slats in the foreground shutters with embroidery, but don't work all of them, just a suggestion of some of them. The flowers on the plants are worked with red French knots.

Voilá! Now your felted picture of a typical French street scene is complete. You can either frame it close around the edge of the picture, or add a cardboard mat in a matching colour, before framing.

Camel

Project 9

This gorgeous camel has lots of braid, embroidery, beading and tassels to embellish his blankets and harness. He has a wire frame, which allows him to stand firmly with such long legs, and his position can also be changed slightly because of the wiring inside him. A wire frame can be used for many different animals, such as bears, horses and dogs. The patterns at the back of the book show the wire outline, the camel outline and the blanket designs.

You will need:
Merino wool sliver Liquorice small piece,
Scarlet 4gm ($1/8$oz), Honey 1gm ($1/32$oz)
Corriedale wool sliver Cookie 100gm ($3 1/2$ozs),
Grey 2gm ($1/16$oz), Lavender small piece
Craft wire 0.9mm (24 gauge)
Pipe cleaners
German glass eyes, 6mm ($1/4$in)
Dental floss for attaching eyes
Water soluble stabiliser
Embroidery cottons, beads, braids, etc
Felting needles 36T, 38S, 40T

Finished size: 22cm ($8 3/4$ins) high

1. Make a wire frame using the pattern as a guide. Bend the legs about 2.5cm (1in) apart at the top to allow for the thickness of the body. Turn under any loose ends of wire so that there are no sharp ends, and then wrap the wire with pipe cleaners. This will make it easier for the wool to grip the wire, instead of slipping.

2. **Body:** Begin by wrapping Cookie wool around the wire base. Wrap firmly around the body and needle lightly to hold, using a 36T needle. Add another layer and needle again to hold it together.

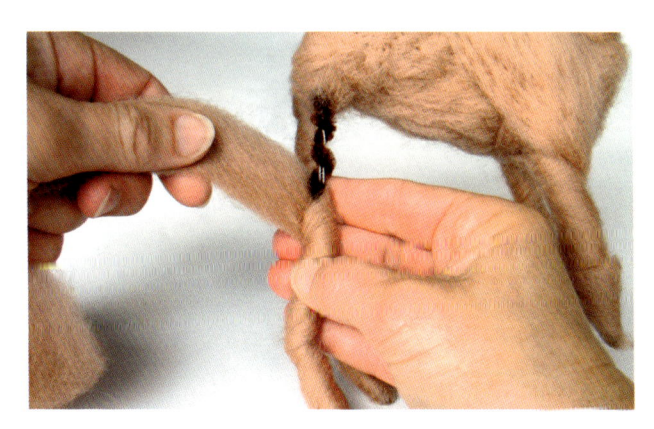

3. At this stage we are not concerned with needle felting the whole way through the body, we just want to stop the wool from unravelling. Push a wad of felted wool into the head shape, and then wrap the neck and head. When doing the legs, make sure they are fairly thin towards the foot.

Camel ... continued

4. Lay extra wool around the top of the thighs to give them fullness. Don't worry about the feet at this stage, we will work them later.

5. Once you have most of the wool in place, begin needle felting thoroughly all over. You will find that your camel will get much thinner as he felts down so add more wool where needed, making sure the edges are feathered out to hide any joins.

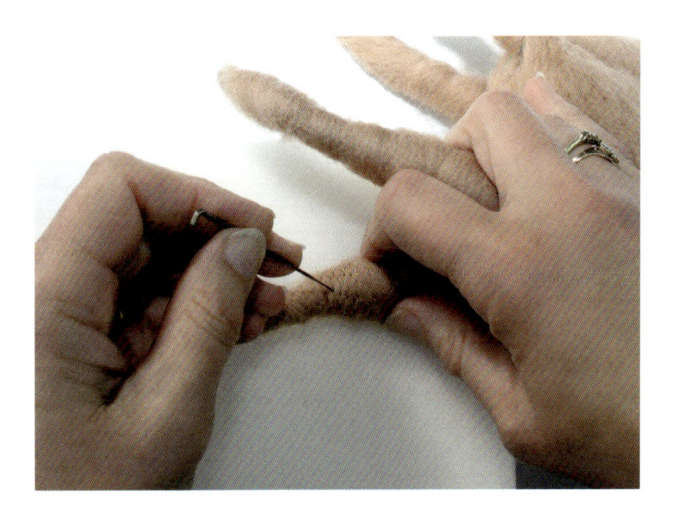

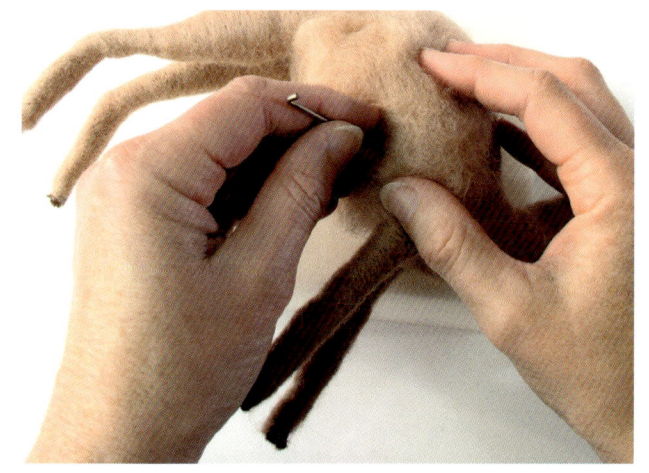

6. Give him a nice high hump for the saddle to sit on, a rounded tummy and a strong chest and neck.

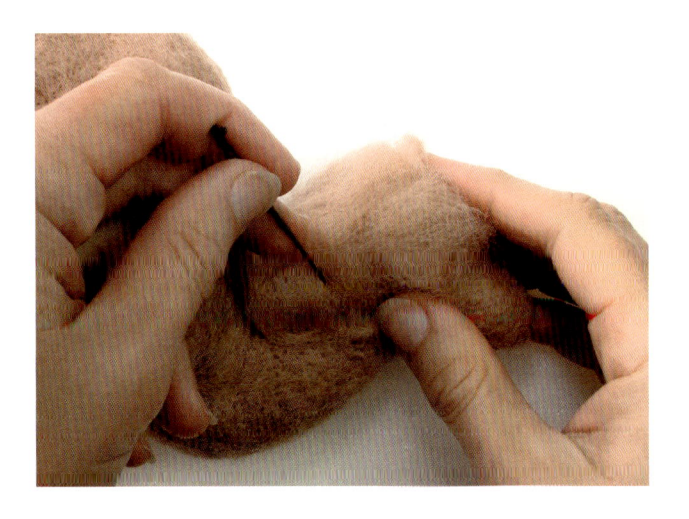

7. Check the shaping by placing your camel over the pattern. Now that the bulky needle felting has been done, change down to a fine needle (40T) for the more detailed work on the rest of the camel.

8. **Legs:** The legs will take some time, as they are thin and you will have to be careful not to catch your needle on the wire inside. You may find it helpful to slide your needle in on a slant, instead of straight up and down.

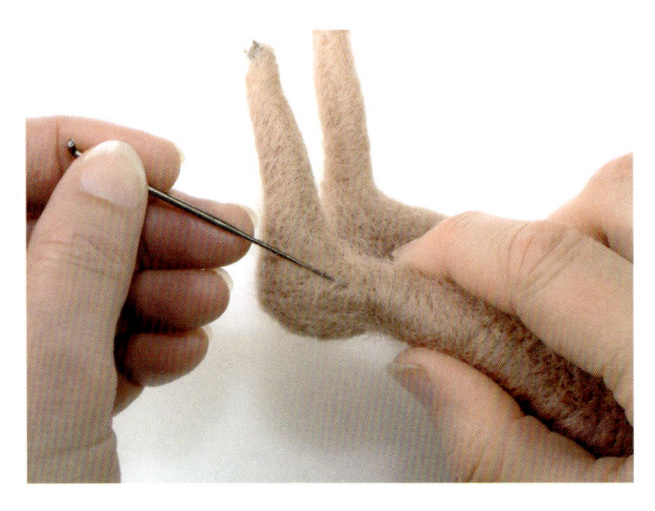

9. Once you have the wrapped wool on the legs felted, add more wool to develop the thighs and back hocks as in the picture, then wrap a little wool around the front legs for the knobbly knees, blending the edges in by feathering.

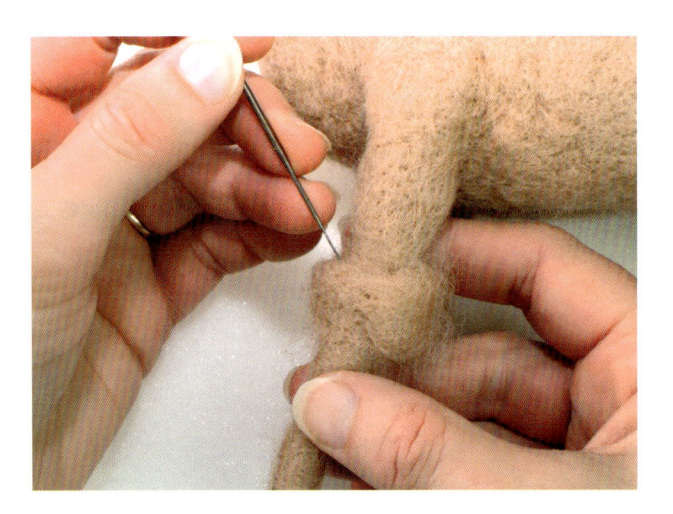

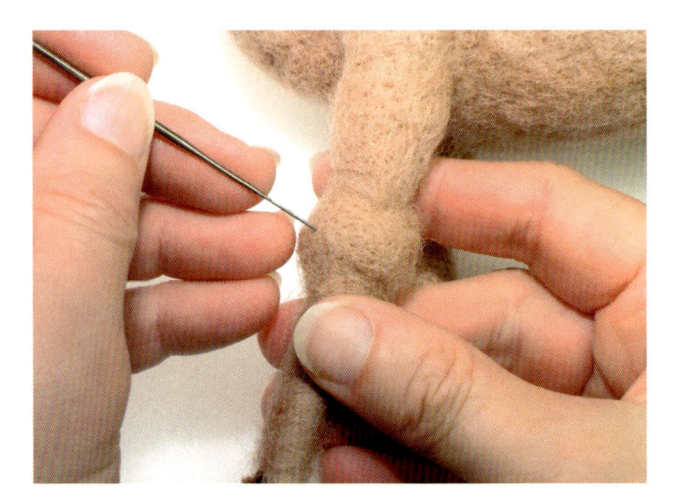

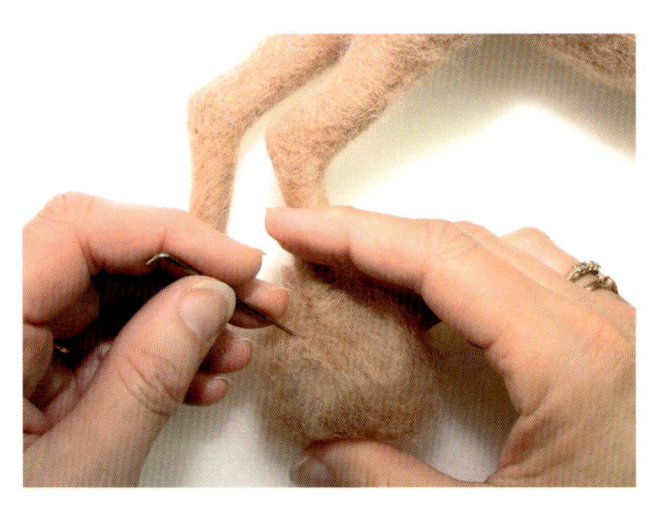

10. Feet: Check that the camel is standing evenly. If not, alter the length of some legs until he is standing straight and not wobbling. Do this by bending the wire in the legs or by adding more wool to the end of a leg.

The camel has a hoof with two toes, so the foot is split up the middle. Pull off four pieces of wool the same size. This will help make the feet the same size when finished. Felt the wool into a loose ball, and then join it to the end of the leg, working around the ankle area until it is firmly attached.

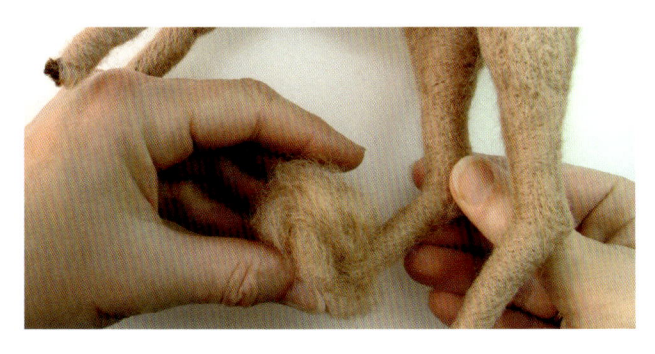

11. Push the wool forward to form the heel then felt the foot firmly.

14. Round over the cut edges with your needle.

12. Notice that a camel's feet are fairly flat not rounded like a teddy bear's.

13. Make sure all the feet are facing forward on the same angle, and then cut them up the middle with scissors, to form the two toes.

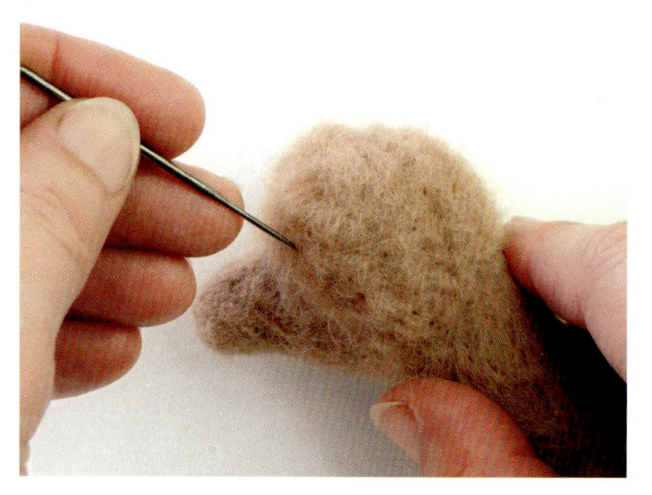

15. Head: Shape the head so it is wider at the back and narrows as it comes forward along the muzzle to the nose.

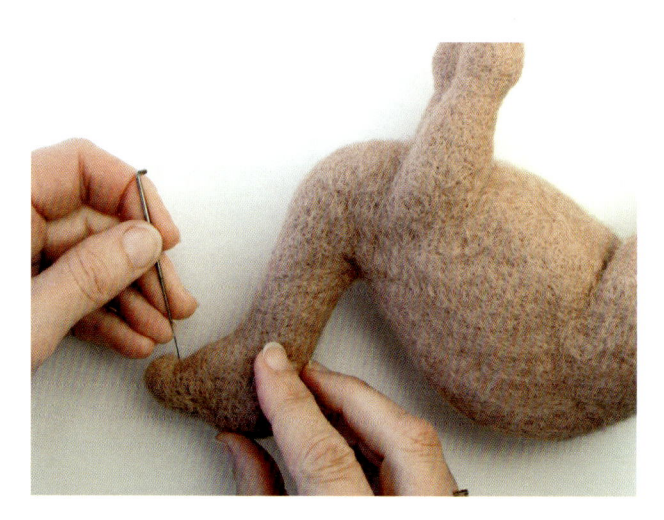

16. Check that the muzzle is long enough, and add more wool if necessary. Needle a dent across the underneath of the jaw, as in the photo. This will help give shape to the lower lip when it is added. Needle underneath the muzzle where the mouth will go, to flatten the muzzle upwards. What we are doing is defining the upper jaw only, so you are forming the upper lip. The lower jaw and lip will be made separately.

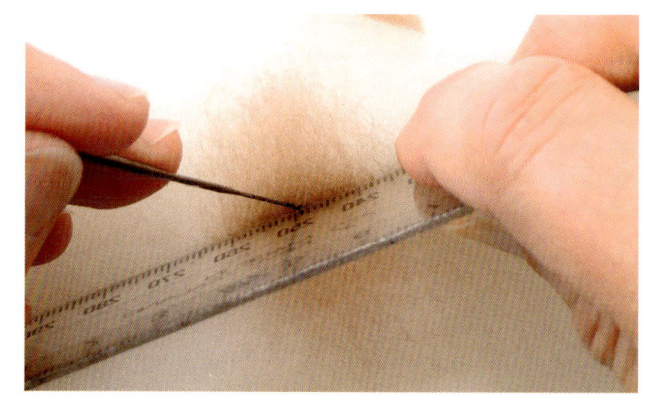

17. Round the top of the muzzle over at the front, and then make the nostrils. Take a small piece of wool and shorten the fibres to about 3cm ($1^1/_2$ins) long. Lay this on the foam, place a straight edge, like a ruler, across the middle and needle a 2.5cm (1in) line across the wool.

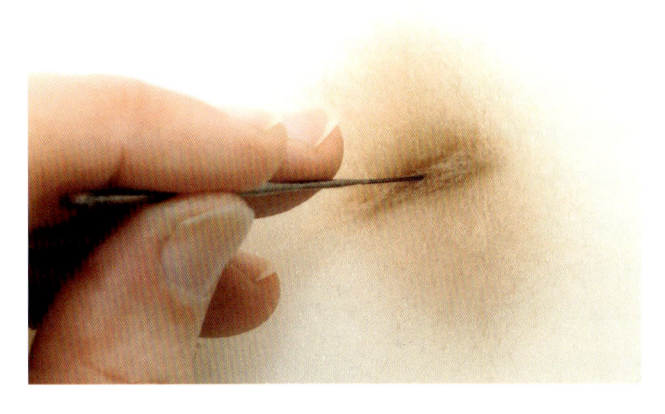

18. Roll a short, thin sausage about the same length as the wool dent and place on top.

20. Now hold the nostril tightly in one hand while you break the wispy ends even shorter, so that the final piece is only about 1cm ($^1/_2$in) wide.

19. Fold the wool over on the line with the sausage inside, and felt down. Lift the piece off the foam and neaten the other side. Continue felting until the edge is firm, leaving the wispy ends loose.

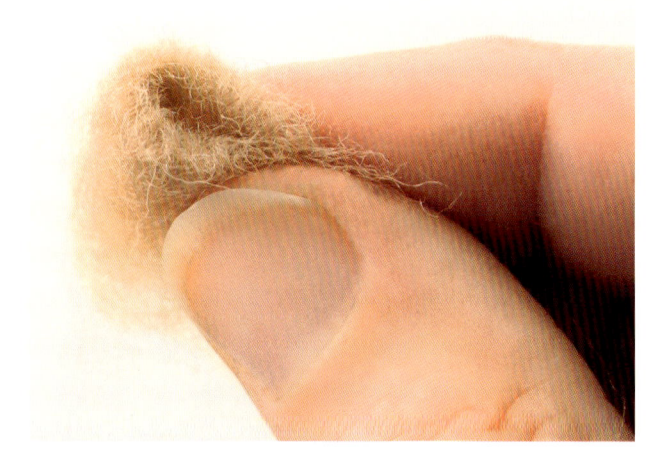

21. If you don't hold tightly, the nostril will break apart when you pull the fibres off. Fold in half and place on the muzzle, with the fold at the back and the join facing forward, and sloped slightly in towards the middle of the muzzle.

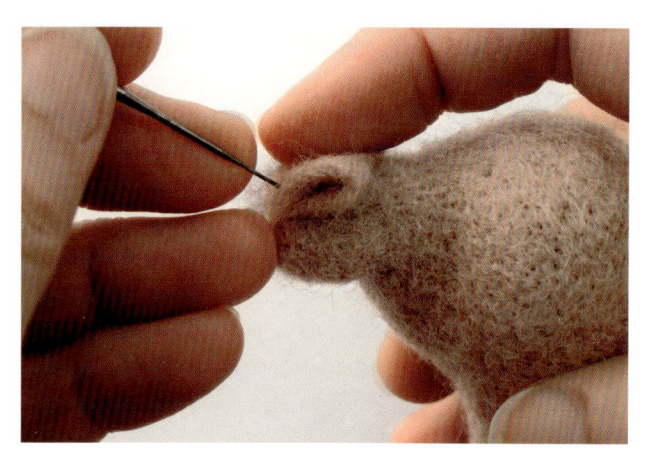

22. Needle the lower half on first, and then the top half, trying not to close the nostril too much, but working all around to attach firmly. Feather out the wispy edges over the top of the muzzle and blend them in. Repeat for the second nostril.

Needle a line from the nose to the upper lip. Then work a shallow dent at each side of the mouth, to continue the line of the mouth back behind the nose.

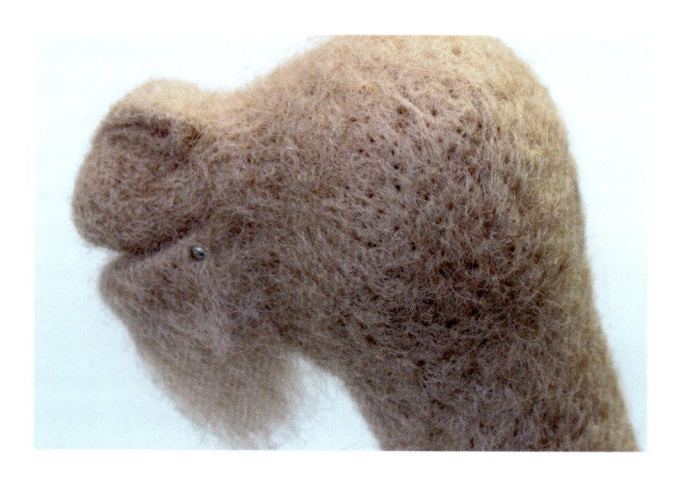

24. Lay some short strands of wool on the foam as for the nostrils, but before needling the dent, check that the width is the same as that of the sausage shape you have just made. Make the dent; fold it over the sausage and needle firmly on the lip area.

23. For the lower lip, repeat the process used for the nostrils, but the lip is wider and thicker. This time make the thin inner sausage shape first to get the right width for the lip. Measure the length of it in position under the upper lip, allowing just the thin wispy ends to extend past the side dents you have added in the above paragraph. Needle until firm.

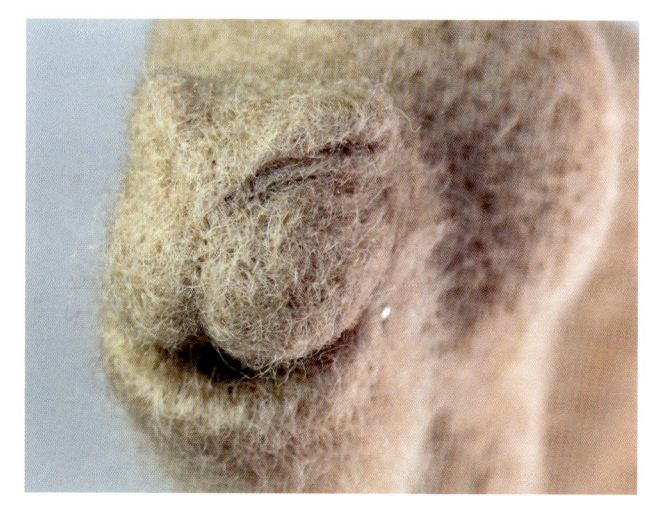

25. Check the length again; it should be about 3.5cm (1½ins) long. Pull off any excess wispy fibres. Position the lower lip so that it is just underneath and back a little from the top lip, attach firmly and work in the wispy fibres.

26. Eyes: Needle a round dent for each eye socket, and then add either black glass eyes (as for the teddybear) or tiny balls of Liquorice wool. If using glass eyes, exit the threads below the opposite ear, covering the dents with tiny wads of wool.

27. Ears: Make a flat square shape 2cm (3/4in) across, then cut in two diagonally to form two small ear triangles.

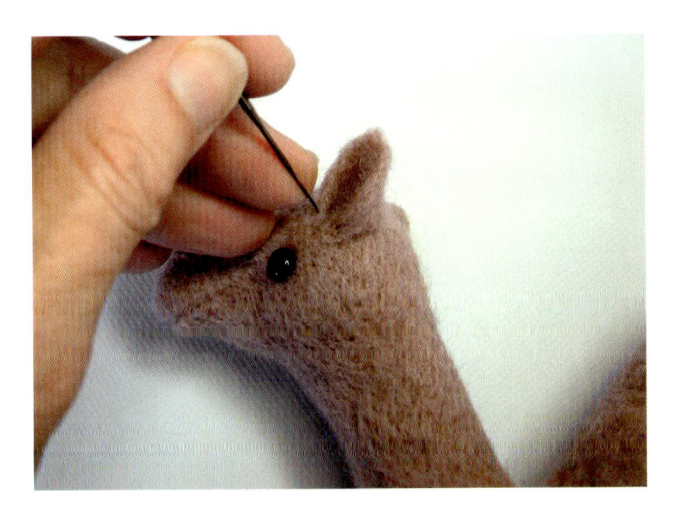

28. Fold each in half and attach on the sides of the head behind the eyes.

29. A camel has very small ears, so keep working on them until they look small enough.

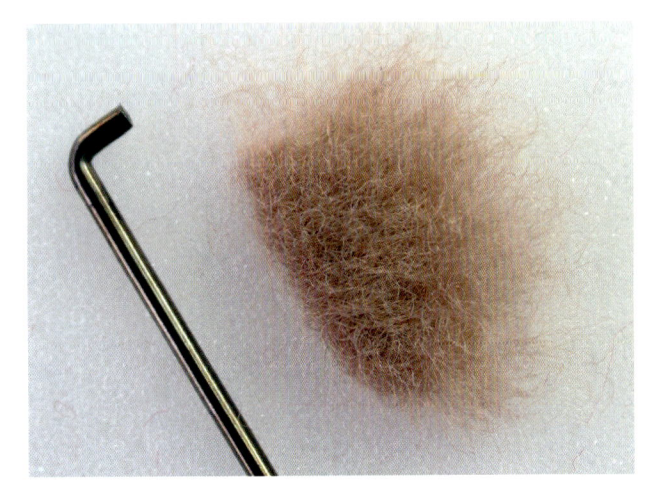

30. Eyelids: Make two small folds of wool for the eyelids. You won't need to add a sausage shape inside the eyelids, just a few flat fibres going across the grain to hold it together when felting. Pull off any excess fibres to make the lid about 2cm (3/4in) wide

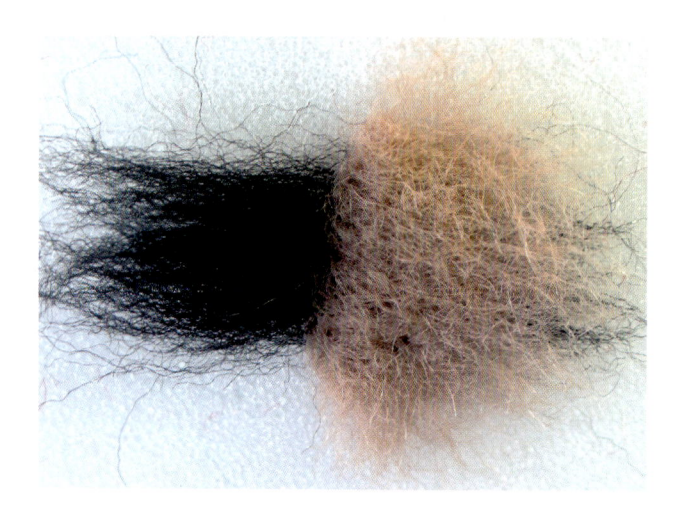

Camel ... continued

31. Add eyelashes by laying short black wool on your foam, about 1cm ($1/2$in) wide, with the fibres all going in the same direction. Place the eyelid on top about halfway along the fibres. Work with your fine needle through the lid and lashes to felt the lid wool down and catch the black wool to it. Work particularly along the edge of the lid.

33. Trim to length when finished, and needle one eyelid over the top of each eye, feathering the remaining wisps over the head. You can see by the photos how these eyelids dramatically alter the expression of the camel.

32. Remove from foam and trim the excess black from underneath the eyelid. Fold the lashes over the outside of the lid and needle them to the edge to help make them curl outward.

34. **Hair:** Our camel has a mop of hair between his ears and coming forward slightly on his forehead. I really enjoy adding the hair; it is so easy and makes such difference to the look of the finished animal. Use a small wad of fibres at a time, but keep them lying flat and parallel instead of mixing them as we usually do.

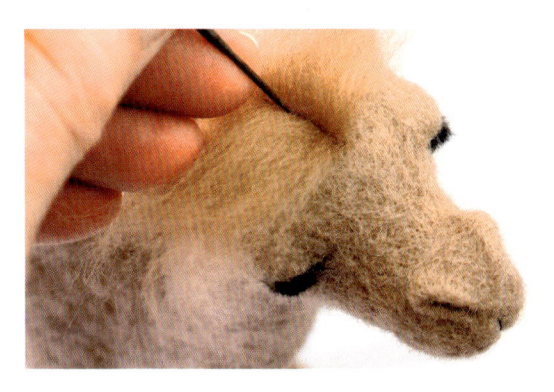

35. Lay the first lot of fibres on top of the head.

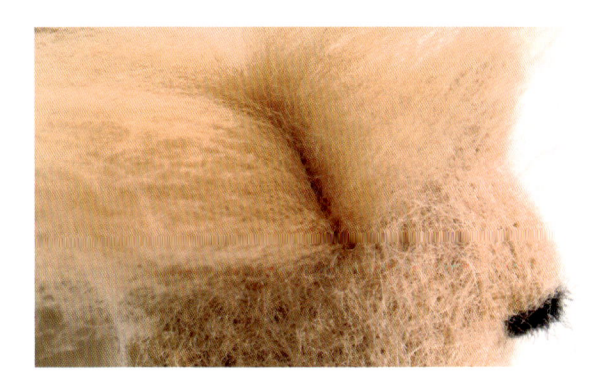

36. Holding the wool with one hand, needle repeatedly in a short line across the middle of these fibres to push them down into the camel's head and embed them, so that when you let go and fold both ends upwards, the hair will stay there.

37. Lay some more wool close to the first lot and to the side, and repeat the process. Do this several times until you have hair embedded all over the top of his head. It should stop just behind his ears and come forward no further than his eyes.

38. At this point your camel will look a bit wild and woolly, so we need to take the scissors to his hair and trim it. You can trim it quite short, as he doesn't have a mane like a horse, rather just a short topknot, really. Don't trim it too short the first time; make several trimmings, checking each time to see if you need to take more off.

Camel ... continued

39. Tail: The tail has a tuft of hair at the end. Take a length of wool twice as long as the finished tuft, with the fibres all running in the same direction. Needle the top half of the wool slightly to hold, and then wrap some mixed wool around it, leaving the end protruding. Needle to form a thin tail.

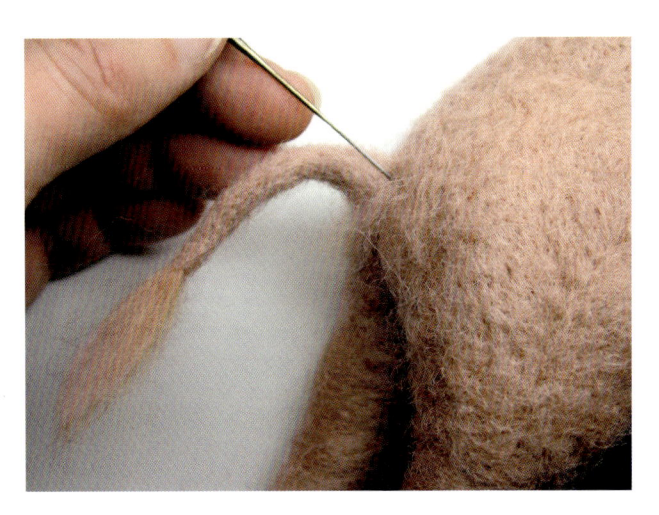

40. Attach this to the rump; note that the position of the tail is quite low.

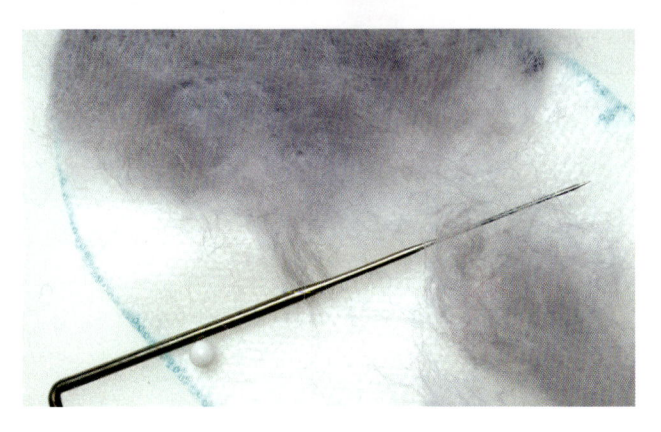

41. Blankets: There are three blankets in all, and the top one is the most lavishly decorated. They are worked with a 38S needle.

42. Grey blanket. Make the rear blanket using Grey wool with Lavender for the pattern on it. This will be a subdued sort of design. Cut the pattern for the blanket out of the stabiliser, and fill it in with Grey wool, keeping the thickness even and not too heavy.

Make a line across the middle with a twisted strand of Lavender wool, securing the end firmly on one side, and then needling thoroughly across the blanket. Cut the wool about .5cm ($^1/_4$in) past the edge, and then work the excess wool back into the blanket. Mark five even lines on each side of the middle with a pin, then work these into stripes like the middle line.

Carefully remove the blanket from the foam, and work in some of the fibres on the back, using your needle on a slant. Rinse to remove the stabiliser and leave to dry flat. Check the size of your blanket against the pattern, as it will probably have stretched during rinsing. If it is too big, shrink it back by working on the back with the felting needle parallel to the surface, working it sideways repeatedly. It won't take much work to reduce it back to size.

Trim any stray fibres then place the blanket on the camel's back between his tail and his hump. Needle it on lightly to keep in place.

43. Red and green blanket. Make the red and green blanket in a similar way. The green can be either needle felted on or embroidered with green thread using stem stitch and fine blanket stitch. I have used a water soluble pen to mark the lines of the pattern.

44. Beaded blanket. The main blanket can be made any way you like. I have needle felted the base on the stabiliser, added a Honey felted stripe, then stitched braid and beading for the pattern, with fringing on the ends.

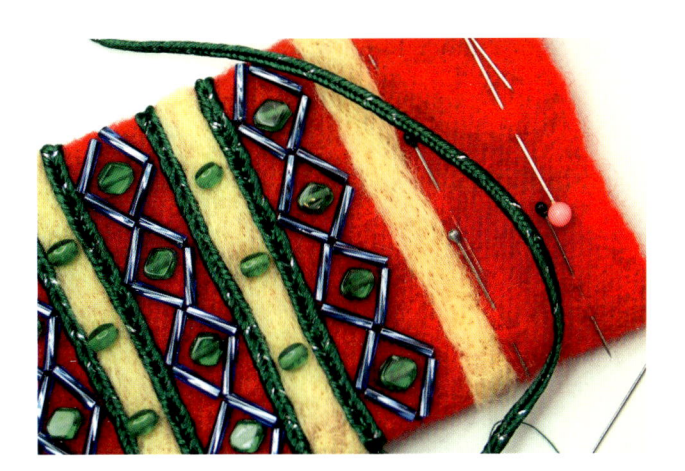

45. Make a pommel from brown wool and attach to the top of the main blanket, so that you can loop the reins over it. Lay the blankets on your camel and needle them lightly to hold in place.

46. Decorating: Make some tiny tassels in lots of bright colours, using embroidery cotton, and hang them off the sides of the camel's neck, just in front of the red blanket. Make a harness from ribbon and braid, decorated with a larger tassel on each side of his cheeks. Attach the reins to this and take them up to the pommel on the saddle.

And that is your camel complete. I am sure he looks quite impressive with all his decoration.

Poppies

Project 10

This brilliantly coloured picture of red poppies in a field of grass will be eye-catching on your wall. It is a combination of flat felting, where we will use colour and shading to define the different petals, and partial 3-D felting of the front flowers to make them pop out of the picture.

I prefer to use Merino wool for flat felting as the fine fibres felt nice and flat, but if this is not available in the colours you need, then Corriedale is fine although a little more wispy.

You will need:
Merino wool sliver Scarlet 12gm ($3/8$oz),
Tangerine 4gm ($1/8$oz), Green Tea 15gm ($1/2$oz),
Beansprout 8gm ($1/4$oz), Liquorice 2gm ($1/16$oz),
White 4gm ($1/8$oz), Lagoon 2gm ($1/16$oz),
Chocolate 2gm ($1/16$oz), Mint 8gm ($1/4$oz)
Corriedale wool sliver Bubblegum 12gm ($3/8$oz),
Chilli Pepper 12gm ($3/8$oz), Pumpkin Pie 2gm ($1/16$oz),
Orange 2gm ($1/16$oz), Lime 8gm ($1/4$oz), Kiwifruit 8gm ($1/4$oz),
Nutmeg 2gm ($1/16$oz))
White flat felt (either wool or acrylic pre-made felt)
Large block of foam
Water soluble stabiliser
Felting needle 38S

Finished size: 42cm (16$1/2$ins) high

The finished size of this picture is A3 or 29.5 x 42cm (11$1/2$ x 16$1/2$ins) w x h. We will establish the background first, then use a second layer of the stabiliser to define the main poppies.

1. Cut the background felt so there is at least a 10 – 15cm (4 – 6ins) border all around the finished picture. With a marker pen draw the outer edges of the picture on to the stabiliser, also the main lines of the sloping hillside and the dark green wool 'frame' on the right side and bottom of the picture. Pin the felt and pattern to a piece of foam at least as large as the finished picture will be.

When working large areas like the sky, lay on small wads of wool, about 3cm (1$1/4$ins) in diameter, working one wad in before laying the next beside the first.

Using a 38S needle felt Bubblegum wool over the whole sky, adding a wispy layer of Lagoon in the top left-hand area for variety, and some White wool representing clouds closer to the horizon. Use a needle punch tool to felt this down thoroughly. Neaten the outside edges, but allow the wool to overflow into the areas where the grass and the dark green frame will be.

Now work the grass. You want it to be paler and less defined near the horizon line, and darker with more definite lines as you come forward to the lower part of the picture.

Blend small wads of Lime and Beansprout wools together, sometimes with a bit of White or Mint, then lay them on the grass area. Starting near the horizon line, needle felt the wool and neaten the edge where it meets the sky.

2. Once this initial area is done, lay the rest of your wool so that the direction of the fibres is running roughly vertical, with some variation in direction to add interest.

4. Fill in the dark green 'frame' with a solid felting of Green Tea. This dark colour will contrast strongly with the red of the flowers to help make them 'pop' out of the picture. There are long straight lines to make all around this frame.

3. This will give more of an impression of grass than if the fibres are going every which way. Place short mixed-colour layers near the horizon (I cut my fibres for the grass about 5cm (2ins) long), overlaying them with darker layers as you move down the picture and varying the colour mixes as you go. Felt the whole area down thoroughly.

5. As you will have lost the inner edges with the overflow of wool from the grass and sky, use a ruler to find them again and poke a row of pins along it, about 3cm ($1^1/_4$ins) apart, then pull the pins out as your work reaches them. You could use the dent-and-fold method to make your straight lines, using a ruler as a straight edge, but I used my 'fingernail facing' method.

6. At the horizon lay in a loose haze of reds to represent the furthest poppies. Use very short fibres for this, about 1 cm ($^1/_2$in), so that you can place them loosely without getting long lines in your work when felting down. Vary the shape and thickness of the wool. Then work down from distant to closer poppies by scattering small spots of Scarlet and Chilli Pepper wool, making them slightly larger and further apart as you move forward in the picture. I placed all these tiny poppies on the left of the picture, as the closer individual poppies we do next will fill in the right side.

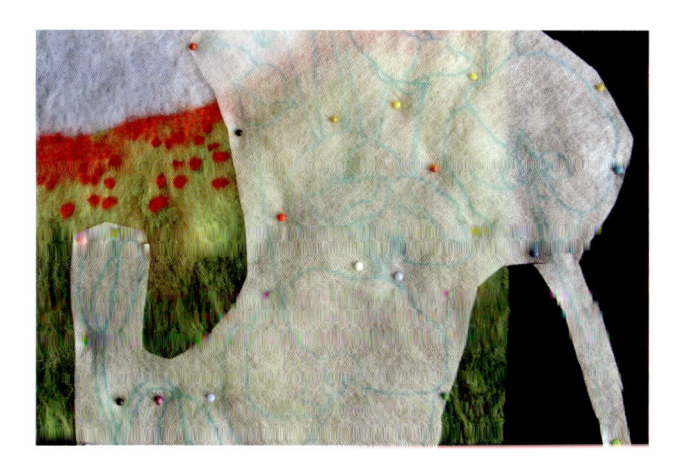

7. To felt the rest of the flowers, trace the pattern onto the stabiliser, omitting the largest flower at the front, which will be felted separately later. Cut roughly around the pattern and pin it to the picture. Work the middle distance flowers on this.

Don't worry about the stabiliser areas between the flowers. This will look strange while you are working but once the flowers are finished, you will rinse the picture in water and it will dissolve, leaving your poppies looking beautiful on their grassy background. Such fun! Water soluble stabilisers give you such versatility in the ways you can use them!

8. To make the flower stalks, use various greens, pulling out a long strand from the wad of mixed wool, twisting it and attaching, using your fingernail to push the wool into place and as a guide for the needle.

Poppies ... continued

9. Fill in the flowers and buds next, varying the colours to provide contrast between one petal and the next. You can mix in Tangerine, Orange, or White with the basic reds to lighten them, and also Chocolate or Green Tea for the shadow areas. Add a spot of Liquorice wool for the black centres and a few wisps of White here and there for highlights.

11. For larger areas, use longer fibres and bigger wads of wool.

10. When blending colours for small areas like the smaller petals, use very short fibres. Having short fibres allows better mixing in a small wad, and by using smaller wads of wool when filling in an area, you also have more control about where the wool is going.

12. Use your fingernail to help neaten up the outside edges of the petals.

13. If your edges get lost once you have worked your underneath petals, just cut out the next petal in stabiliser and pin in place, then felt over the top until it is hidden. As long as you felt thoroughly, you won't even know that the stabiliser is underneath.

15. The buds are made slightly rounded over the surface, so you may find it best to work a sausage shape on a separate piece of foam, then felt it in position, before covering with your final layer of colour and shading.

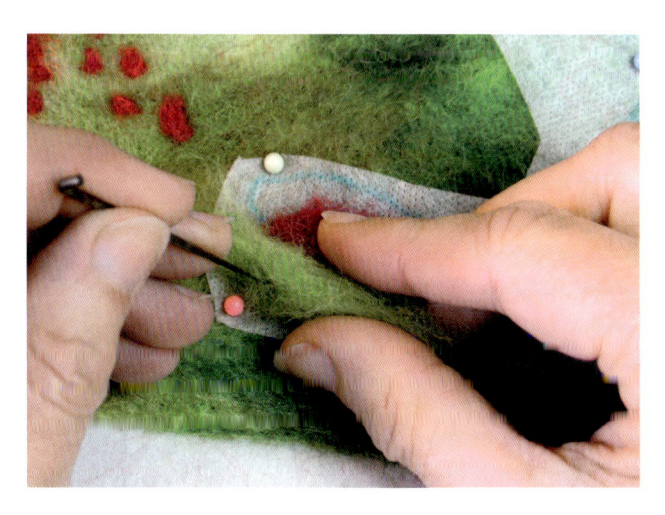

14. Now work on the two foreground buds, and the right hand poppy facing away.

16. Stay aware of the colours in the background behind the poppies and try to make them dark against light colours, and light against dark.

The Ashford Book of Needle Felting 85

17. When you have finished flat felting the right hand poppy facing away, make the stem and sepals slightly 3-D so they sit on the surface, instead of flat.

18. While working on the stem don't let it get too wide as you build it up. Use your fingernail or a small ruler to push the edges back towards the middle of the stem as you work.

19. For the centre poppy, fill in the background petals first. They will look a bit strange on their own, but once the top petals are added later the poppy will look fine.

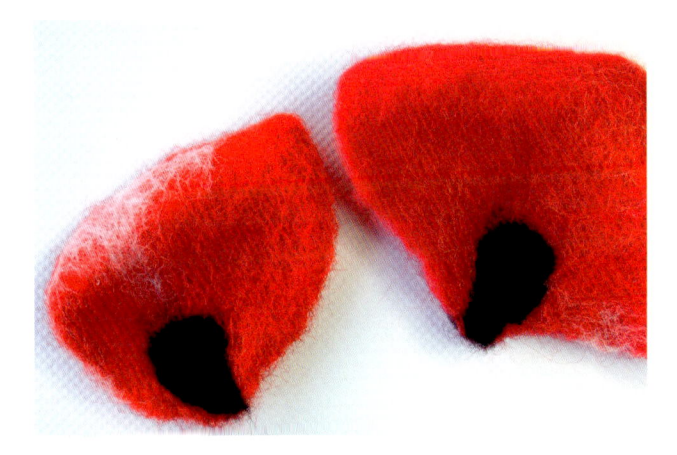

20. Make the top two petals separately. Trace the pattern pieces onto the stabiliser and cut them out, leaving a margin around the edges for pinning to the foam block. Needle a thin layer of wool over each petal until the pattern is completely covered. As with the iris, you don't want the flower to look too thick, but this time it needs to be just thick enough so that it is not see-through. Add some shading and the black central spots. Rinse in warm water, pat dry on a towel, and then shape the petals so that they are folding back along the edges a little and there is a forward curve in the black spot area. Allow to dry, and put them aside for now.

21. Give the work a final thorough felting to make sure everything is well attached (particularly the edges of the poppies felted on top of the stabiliser), then carefully remove from foam and rinse the picture in warm water until the stabiliser is dissolved.

Dry between two towels, then leave to dry flat before continuing. Check the picture now to see if you have enough colour contrast between the green stems and buds, and the background. If not, add a little colour to help make them stand out.

Needle the two petals to the centre poppy so that some of the petal is felted flat and some parts are poking forward from the picture. Make a round Beansprout centre for the poppy and felt on, allowing it to be a 3-D bump instead of flat.

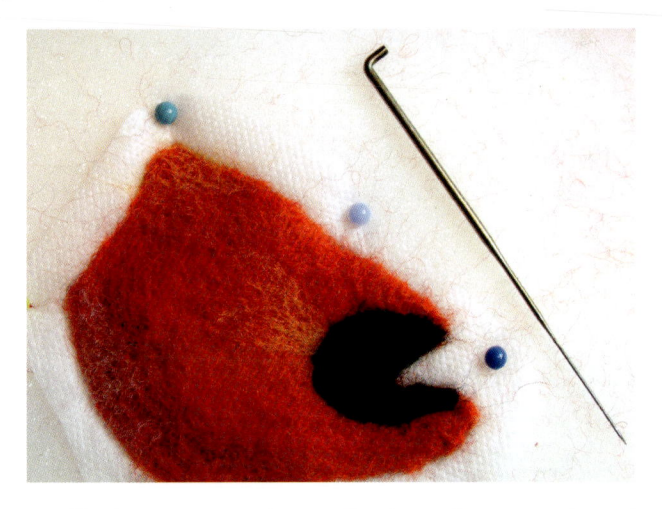

22. The largest poppy is completely made separately and then felted to the picture, so that most of the flower is 3-D and appears to be popping right out of the picture. The petals can even extend past the edge of the picture a little to emphasise its 3-dimensional quality.

Use the stabiliser for the petals and make them thick enough so that the dark green background won't show through. You don't need to vary the colours on the first petal as most of it will be covered by others. Notice that these petal patterns have a dart at the base. Needle the wool around these darts, don't cut them out later. If you cut them the fibres will be too short to join together when the petal is finished.

Make all the petals, varying the colours of wool, giving them highlights with a bit of White or Tangerine. Tease out the edges where the different colours meet so that there are no hard lines and add the black centre spots.

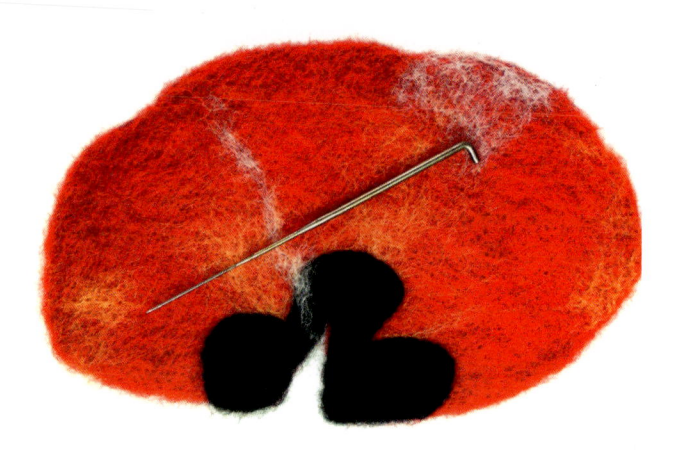

23. When the petals are finished, rinse them and pat dry with a towel. While still damp, tidy up the edges by working any stray fibres back into the petal, then check the petal against the pattern for size.

24. You will probably find that it is a little larger than the pattern since the stabiliser has been removed. It is an easy matter to shrink the petals back to size by holding a felting needle flat, parallel to the work and pushing the needle in sideways. Keep needling inwards from all sides until the work is back to the right size.

25. Now overlap the sides of each dart together and needle the fibres until joined. This will give your petals a nice curve at the base. To persuade the outer part to curve over, work across the petal on the back surface with your felting needle on a slant. What you are doing is shortening the back but not the front surface, so that it curves over. Bend the petals in the final shape you want and leave to dry over a roll of wool sliver.

26. You are now ready to position the poppy on your picture. Pin the petals in place first to check the positioning then felt them on, one at a time. Needle about one third of each petal on to the background. Petals one and two should be beside each other, with petal three on top of two. The top petals, four and five, wrap around each other slightly on the left side.

27. When you attach these, only needle about one quarter of their surface, so that they are able to stand out more than the others. A round ball of Beansprout for the centre, a few stitches of black thread and a French knot in the middle will complete the poppy.

And there you have it! Finished! Your beautiful poppy picture can either be framed, or hung as a wall hanging by attaching a bar to the top of it.

Project patterns

Enlarge patterns to the finished size

7.8 x 12.3cm
(3 x 4$^3/_4$ins) w x h
Enlarge 125%

7.4 x 5.5cm (3 x 2$^1/_4$ins) w x h
Enlarge 125%

15.3 x 7.8cm (6 x 3ins) w x h 100%

Teddybear

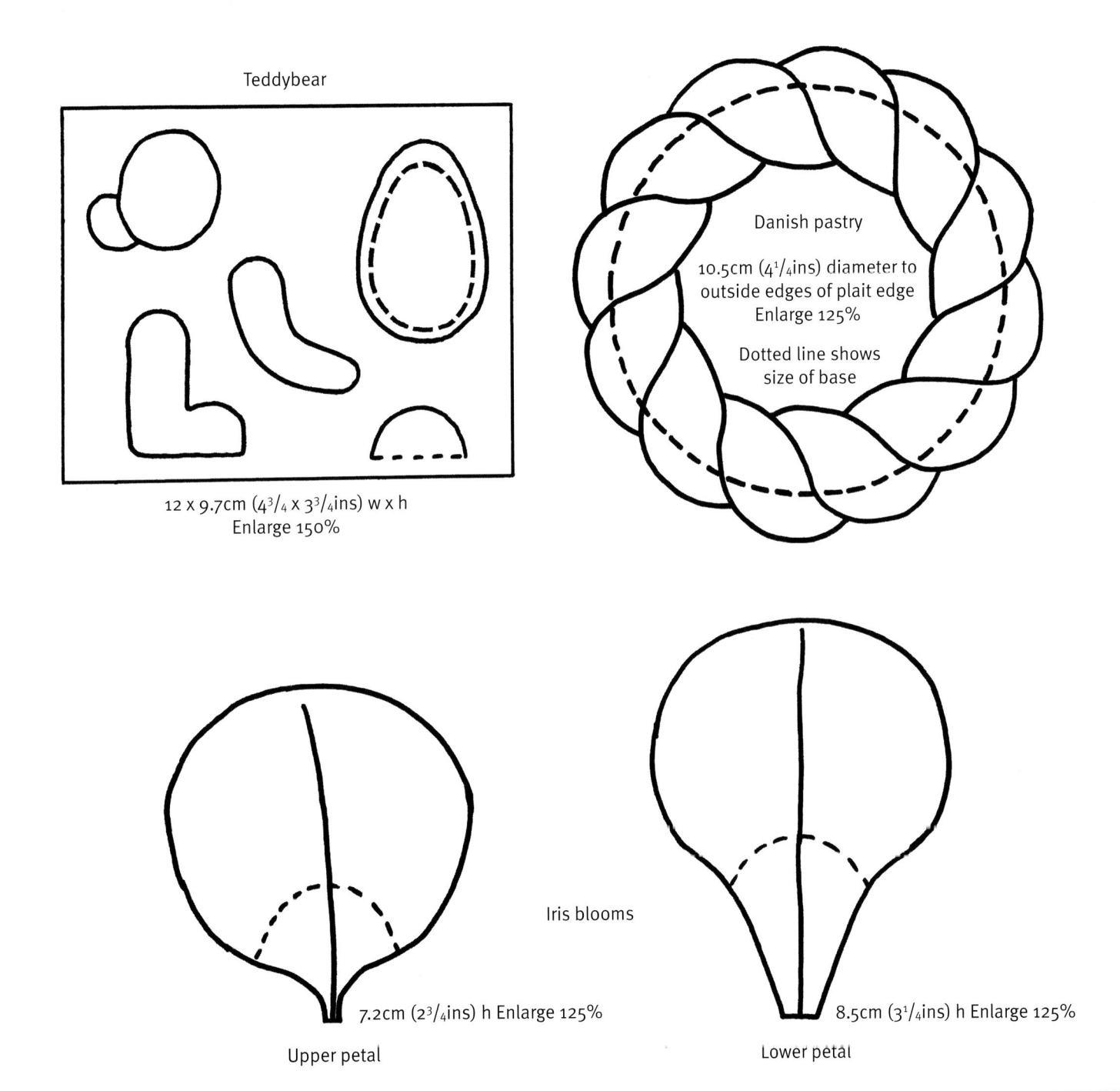

12 x 9.7cm (4¾ x 3¾ins) w x h
Enlarge 150%

Danish pastry

10.5cm (4¼ins) diameter to outside edges of plait edge
Enlarge 125%

Dotted line shows size of base

Iris blooms

7.2cm (2¾ins) h Enlarge 125%

Upper petal

8.5cm (3¼ins) h Enlarge 125%

Lower petal

Project patterns ... continued

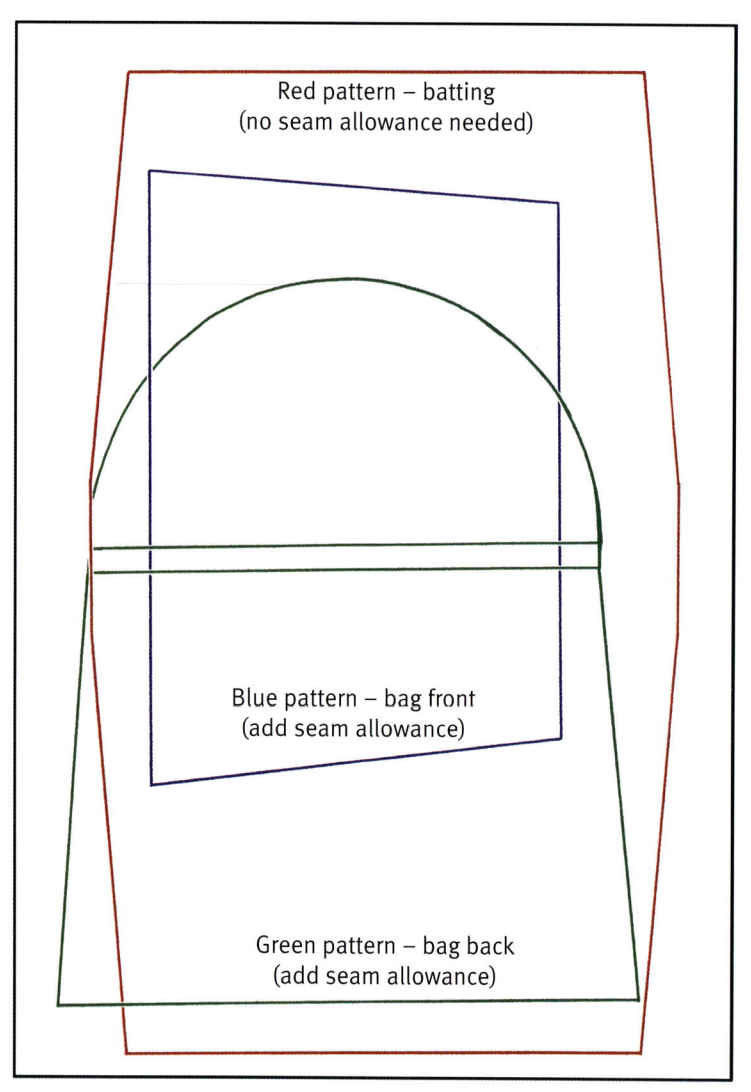

Red pattern – batting
(no seam allowance needed)

Blue pattern – bag front
(add seam allowance)

Green pattern – bag back
(add seam allowance)

29.6 x 42cm (11½ x 16½ins) w x h
Enlarge 300%

Straight edge 21.3cm (8½ins)
Enlarge 200%

21 x 29.5cm (8¼ x 11½ins) w x h
Enlarge 200%

Project patterns ... continued

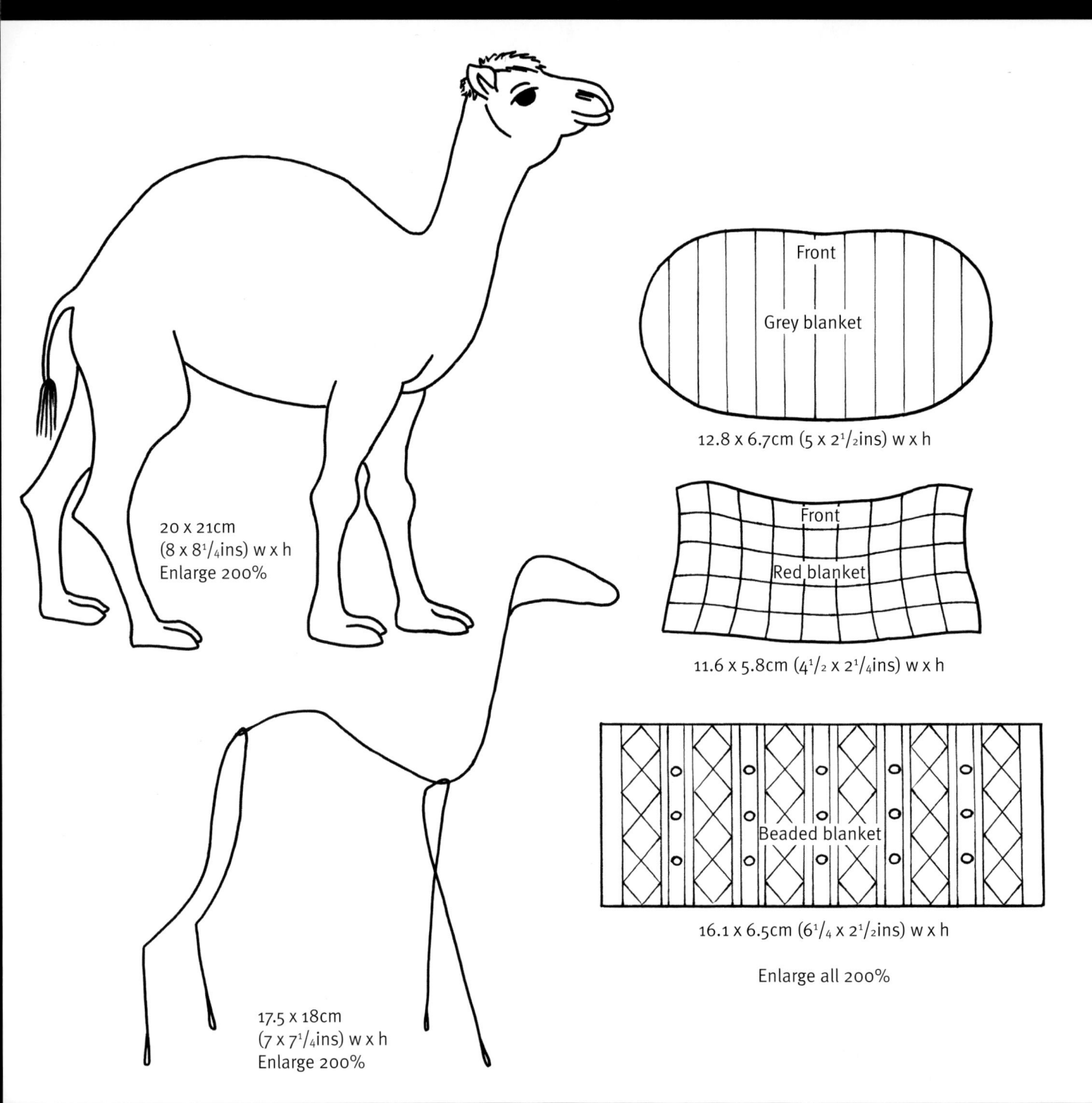

20 x 21cm
(8 x 8¼ins) w x h
Enlarge 200%

Front
Grey blanket

12.8 x 6.7cm (5 x 2½ins) w x h

Front
Red blanket

11.6 x 5.8cm (4½ x 2¼ins) w x h

Beaded blanket

16.1 x 6.5cm (6¼ x 2½ins) w x h

Enlarge all 200%

17.5 x 18cm
(7 x 7¼ins) w x h
Enlarge 200%

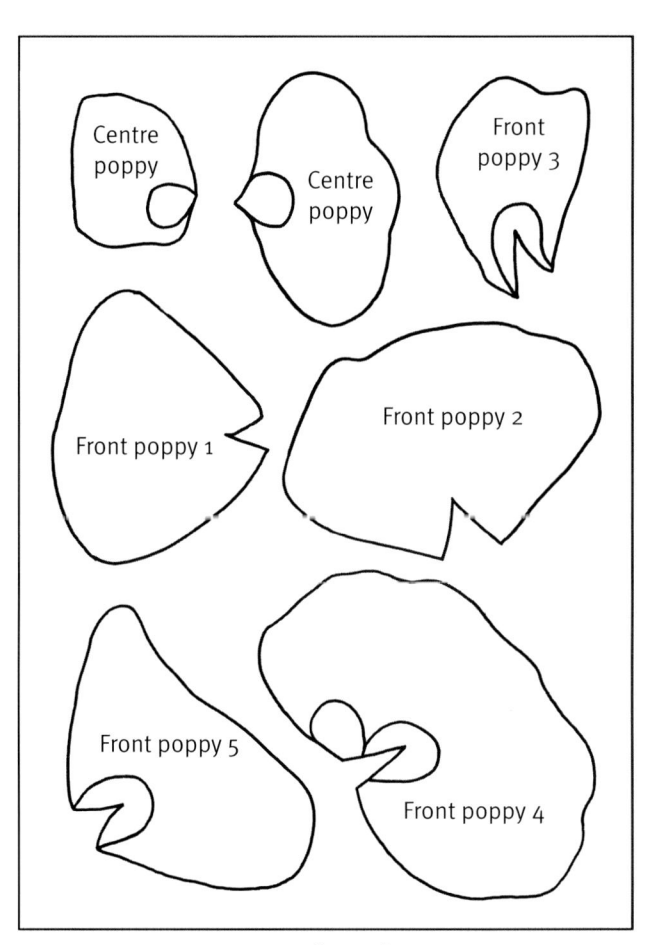

Centre poppy

Centre poppy

Front poppy 3

Front poppy 1

Front poppy 2

Front poppy 5

Front poppy 4

21 x 29.5cm (8¼ x 11½ins) w x h
Enlarge 250%

29.5 x 42cm (11½ x 16½ins) w x h
Enlarge 300%

Gallery

I do hope you have enjoyed working through the projects in this book, and will be inspired to continue experimenting with the wonderful possibilities of needle felting as you browse through the pictures in this Gallery. Happy felting!

Flower brooch
A simple but effective flower made with two separate layers that are needle felted together when finished.

Mouse/hedgehog
Formed from a basic cone shape, with limbs added, he can be changed dramatically with the addition of either a wired tail to create a mouse, or bristles for a hedgehog. You could try different ears and tail for a variety of animals.

Baby pinafore
A cute pink rabbit needle felted onto a corduroy baby's pinafore. Characters like this can create unique decorations on your children's clothing.

Picture frames
Let your imagination run wild in decorating pictures for framing or scrapbooking. The old-fashioned study is printed on photo paper while the little boy over the page is a photo printed on fabric. With the addition of fibres, lace, buttons, beads and butterflies you can create your own personalised frames.

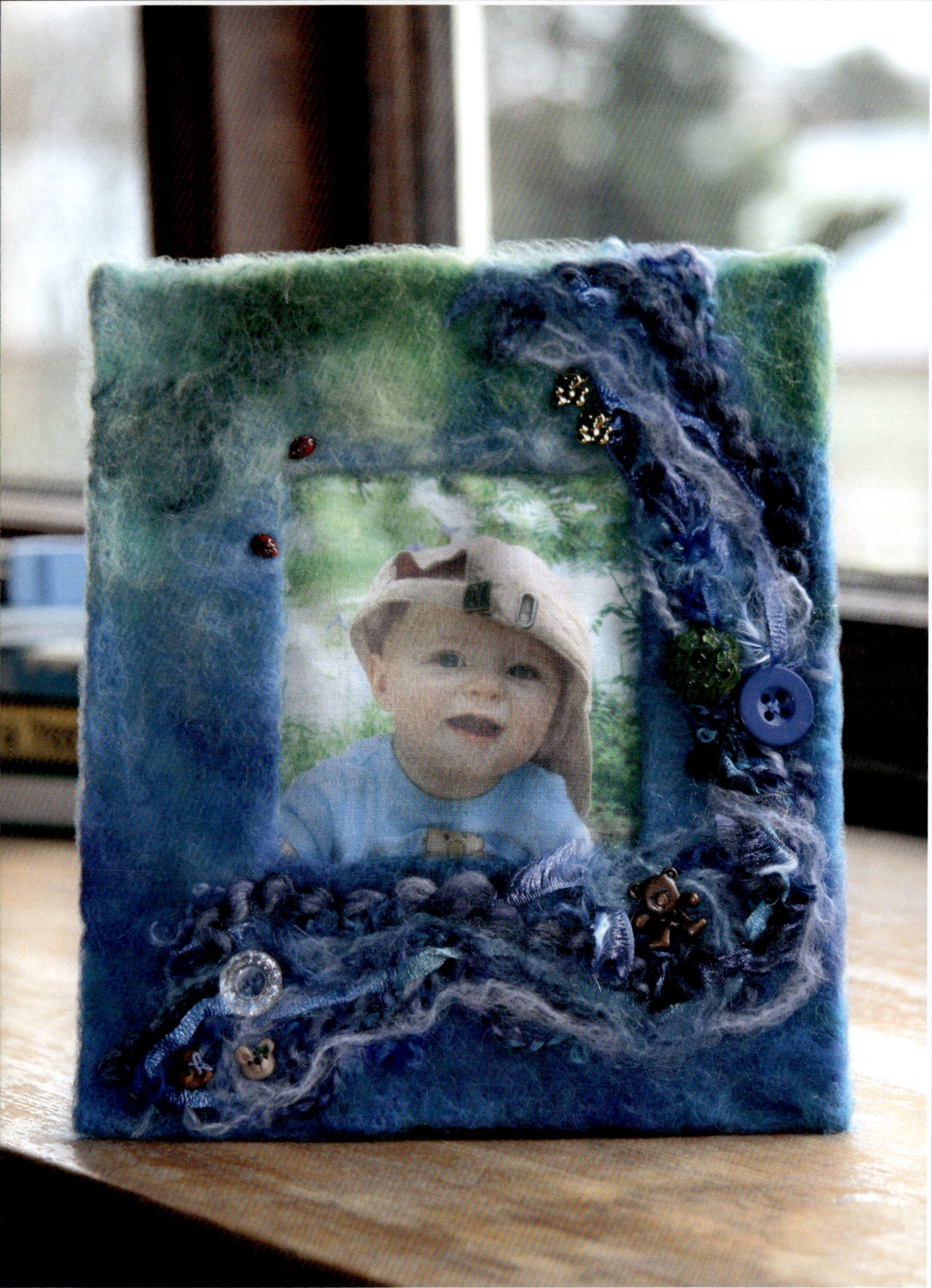

Lambs
These cute lambs have no armature inside, they are just solid felt all the way through.

Appliqué cushion
Flat felting used as appliqué on a cotton cushion. Needle felted appliqué can be large and bold like this, or small and finely detailed.

Dog
This Beagle is felted over a wire armature so that the legs and head can be moved slightly for posing.

Noah's Ark

This wall hanging, felted onto a blue felt background, is full of fun animals and will delight some lucky child. The combination of flat and 3-D felting adds interest; the child can lift the elephant's ear to see behind it, feel the fluffy mane on the lion, and run his hands over the rest of the raised or flat features.

Needle felted figures
Needle felted people are a lot of fun to make, and not as hard as you would think. These are softly felted so they can be bent and posed.

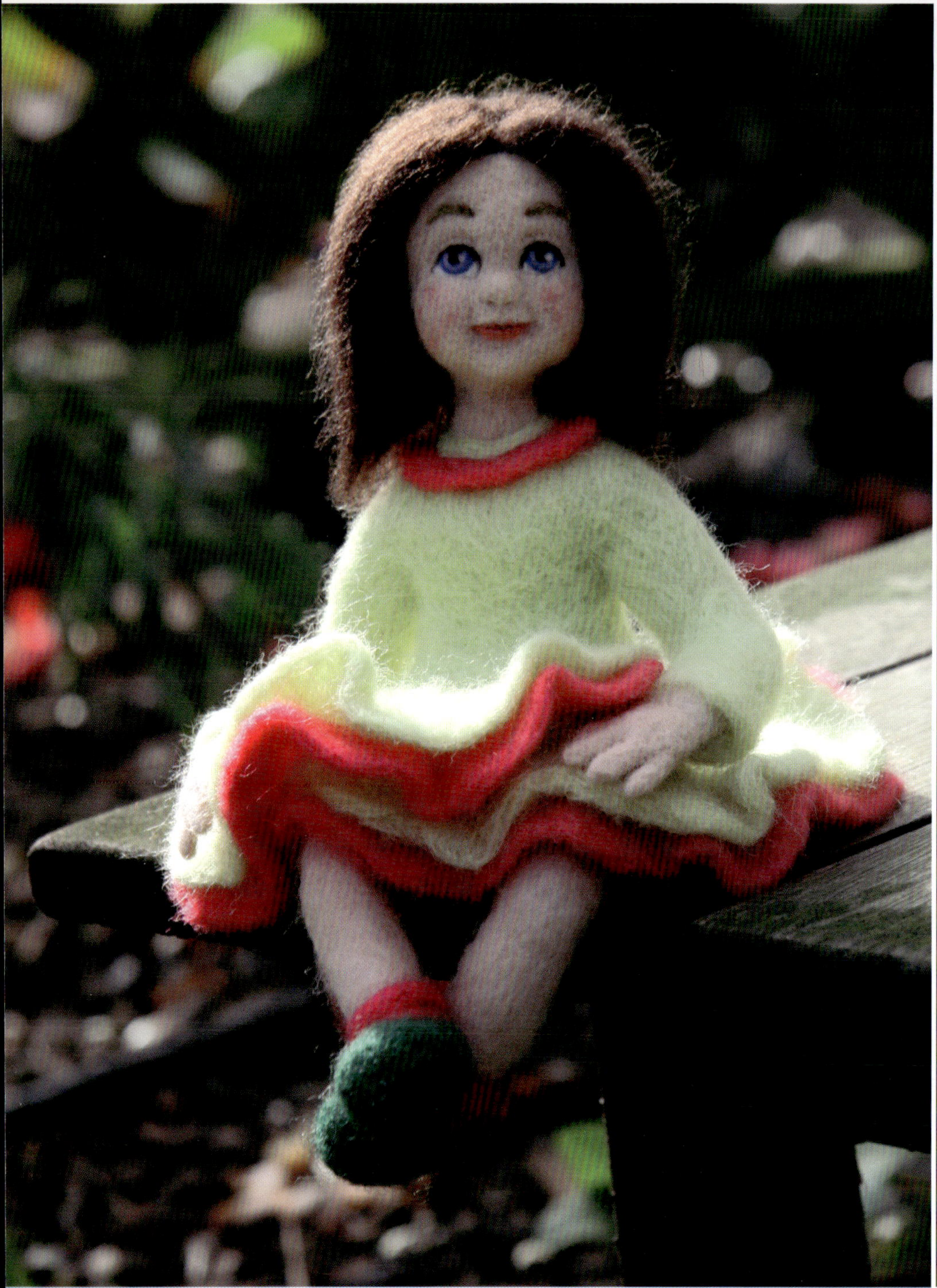

Alpaca jacket
A gorgeous, unique denim jacket. Use a picture of your favourite pet or hobby; there are endless possibilities here.

Appliqué floral quilt
Made as a wall hanging, the appliqué on this quilt is totally done in needle felting. You can add a great deal of detailed shading into your flowers like this, or even a little 3-D for greater effect. Finished size 90cm (35½ins) square

Mother and baby
My daughter and granddaughter! This was such an interesting picture to create, stretching the limits of needle felting. Portraying the highlights and shadows was a challenge. Worked from a photograph, this is a picture to frame and treasure.

Ashford sliver colours

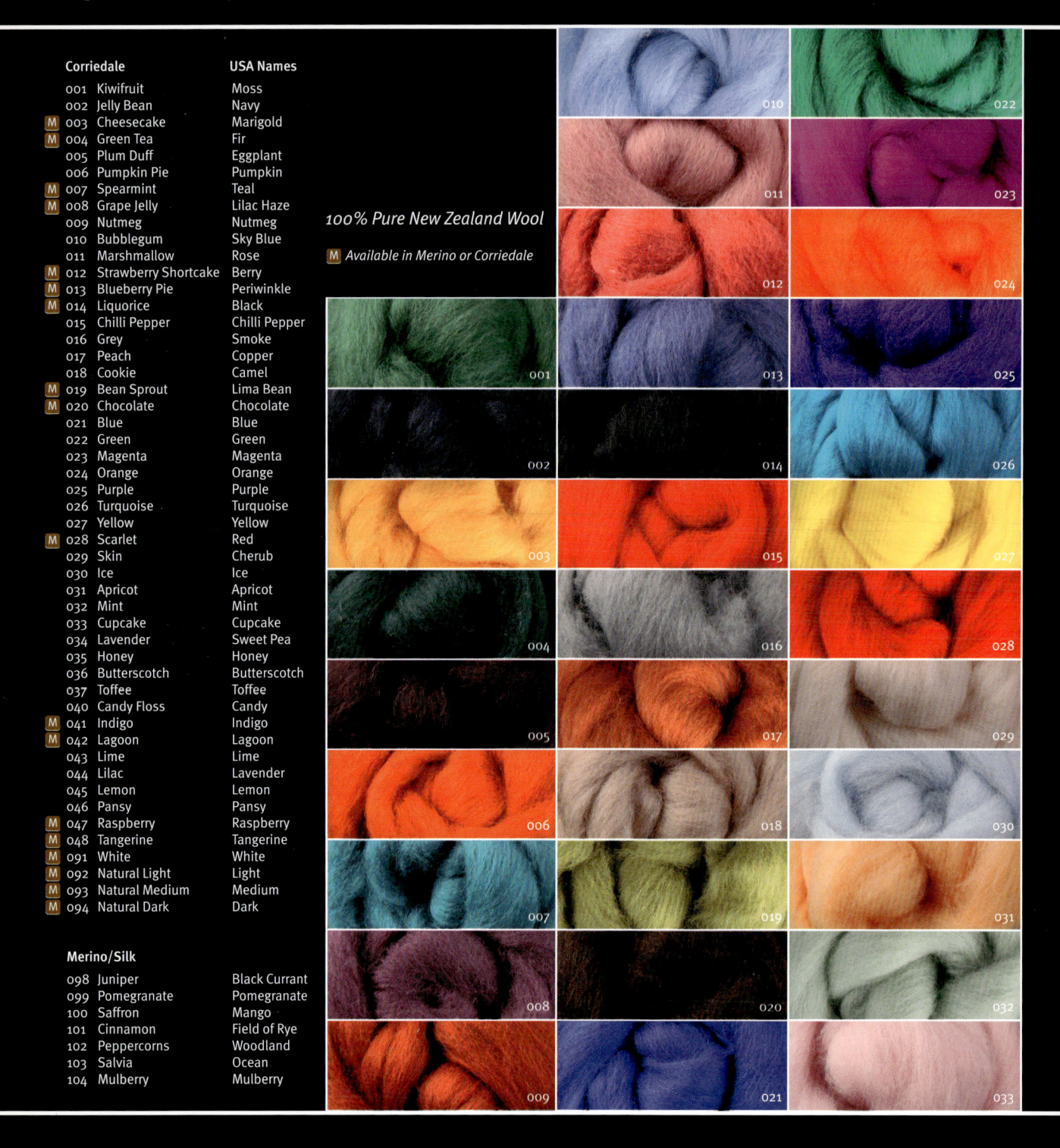

100% Pure New Zealand Wool

M Available in Merino or Corriedale

	Corriedale	USA Names
	001 Kiwifruit	Moss
	002 Jelly Bean	Navy
M	003 Cheesecake	Marigold
M	004 Green Tea	Fir
	005 Plum Duff	Eggplant
	006 Pumpkin Pie	Pumpkin
M	007 Spearmint	Teal
M	008 Grape Jelly	Lilac Haze
	009 Nutmeg	Nutmeg
	010 Bubblegum	Sky Blue
	011 Marshmallow	Rose
M	012 Strawberry Shortcake	Berry
M	013 Blueberry Pie	Periwinkle
M	014 Liquorice	Black
	015 Chilli Pepper	Chilli Pepper
	016 Grey	Smoke
	017 Peach	Copper
	018 Cookie	Camel
M	019 Bean Sprout	Lima Bean
M	020 Chocolate	Chocolate
	021 Blue	Blue
	022 Green	Green
	023 Magenta	Magenta
	024 Orange	Orange
	025 Purple	Purple
	026 Turquoise	Turquoise
	027 Yellow	Yellow
M	028 Scarlet	Red
	029 Skin	Cherub
	030 Ice	Ice
	031 Apricot	Apricot
	032 Mint	Mint
	033 Cupcake	Cupcake
	034 Lavender	Sweet Pea
	035 Honey	Honey
	036 Butterscotch	Butterscotch
	037 Toffee	Toffee
	040 Candy Floss	Candy
M	041 Indigo	Indigo
M	042 Lagoon	Lagoon
	043 Lime	Lime
	044 Lilac	Lavender
	045 Lemon	Lemon
	046 Pansy	Pansy
M	047 Raspberry	Raspberry
M	048 Tangerine	Tangerine
M	091 White	White
M	092 Natural Light	Light
M	093 Natural Medium	Medium
M	094 Natural Dark	Dark

Merino/Silk

	098 Juniper	Black Currant
	099 Pomegranate	Pomegranate
	100 Saffron	Mango
	101 Cinnamon	Field of Rye
	102 Peppercorns	Woodland
	103 Salvia	Ocean
	104 Mulberry	Mulberry

About the author

My husband and I live in New Zealand on a small block of land in a lovely old 1930's home called Cobweb Cottage. I have always considered myself a painter more than anything, and painting in watercolours and oils is still my greatest love. But over the last few years needle felting has taken over my life and I am still fascinated with what can be done with this craft. The more you experiment with needle felting, the more possibilities open up.

I first learnt needle felting in 2002, and was immediately excited by it. Housework became neglected as I sat all day felting teddybears. I already had a small web-based business selling miniature velvet teddybears, and soon needle felted bears and needle felting supplies were selling well too.

As I began teaching others I realised that there was a great need for an instruction book. So early in 2004 my first book was published, 'Needlefelting Magic: Making Beautiful Teddybears'. I was overwhelmed with the response to this; it sold well all over the world and is still in demand today.

Being asked by Ashfords to write another book has given me the opportunity to push the boundaries of needle felting even further, exploring many different ways of using this incredible craft. I hope these projects will appeal not only to beginners but also to more experienced needle felters, broadening your ideas on the possibilities of needle felting.

Barbara's Website: www.cobwebcottage.co.nz

Acknowledgements:

I would like to thank designer Craig McKenzie, Tina Gill for her superb photography and her husband Dan for modelling the vest. Also Elizabeth Ashford for her constant encouragement and guidance. And lastly, my husband Ian for his patience and support in keeping house and home running while I have been busy writing.

Ashford distributors

NEW ZEALAND:
Ashford Handicrafts Limited
PO Box 474, Ashburton
Tel: (+64-3) 308 9087
Fax: (+64-3) 308 8664
email: sales@ashford.co.nz
www.ashford.co.nz

AUSTRALIA:
Ashford Handicrafts Limited
PO Box 474, Ashburton, NZ
FreePh: (1800) 653 397
Free Fax: (1800) 652 290
email: sales@ashford.co.nz
www.ashford.co.nz

AUSTRIA:
Wiener Webwaren
Vienna
Tel: (+43-1) 292 7108
email: info@wienerwebwaren.at
www.wienerwebwaren.at

CANADA:
Harmonique Spinning Wheels & Looms
Victoria, BC
Tel:(+1-250) 294 4411
Fax:(+1-250) 294 8411
email: info@harmonique.ca
www.harmonique.ca

CHILE:
Sociedad Commercial Wisniak
Santiago
Tel: (+56-2) 5569221
Fax: (+56-2) 5516519
email: losalata@interaccess.cl
www.costuritas.cl

CZECH REPUBLIC:
Dalin Praha Sro
Praha
Tel: (+420-2) 74860304
Fax: (+420-2) 74860304
email: dlinhartova@dalin-praha.cz
www.dalin-praha.cz

DENMARK:
Skytten
4871 Horbelev
Tel:(+45) 5444 5020
Fax:(+45) 5444 5022
email:mail@skytten-danmark.dk

FRANCE:
Ets P Marie Saint Germain
Remiremont, Cedex
Tel:(+33 3) 29 23 00 48
Fax:(+33 3) 29 23 20 70
email: contact@artifilum.com
www.artifilum.com

HOLLAND:
The Spinners
Den Haag
Tel:(+31-7) 0397 3643
email: boer381@zonnet.nl
www.despinners.nl

JAPAN:
Ananda Co Limited
Yamanashi
Tel:(+81-551) 32 4215
Fax:(+81-551) 32 4830
email: wool@ananda.jp
www.ananda.jp

Craft Hitsujiza
Fukuoka-shi
Tel:(+81-92) 8511 358
Fax:(+81-92) 8511 358

La Mer Co Ltd
Kyoto
Tel:(+81-75) 634 5942
Fax:(+81-75) 634 5943
email: lamer@joy.ocn.ne.jp

Mariya Handicrafts Limited
Sapporo
Tel:(+81-11) 221 3307
Fax:(+81-11) 232 0393
email: koichi-m@ra2.so-net.ne.jp

Sanyo Trading Company Limited
Ibaraki
Tel:(+81) 297 78 1000
Fax:(+81) 297 78 5850
email: adx01490@ams.odn.ne.jp

MALAYSIA:
Multifilla (M) Sdn BHD
Selangor Darul Ehsan
Tel: (+60-3) 89613686
Fax: (+60-3) 89613637
email: mfilla@tm.net.my
www.multifilla.com

NORWAY:
Spinninger
Billingstad
Tel:(+47) 66 84 60 22
Fax:(+47) 66 84 60 22

REPUBLIC OF KOREA:
LDH Hand Weaving Loom
Fine Corp Ltd
Seoul
Tel:(+82-2) 779 1894
Fax:(+82-2) 755 1663
email: finecenter@finecenter.com
www.finecenter.com

SOUTH AFRICA:
Campbell Crafts & Marketing
Cape Town
Tel:(+27) 21 686 6668
Fax:(+27) 21-448 8506
email: campbellcrafts@netactive.co.za

SWEDEN:
Gudruns Ullbod
Enkoping
Tel:(+46-171) 399 95
Fax:(+46-171) 399 96
email: ullbod@gudrunsullbod.com

SWITZERLAND:
Spycher-Handwerk
Huttwil
Tel:(+41-629) 62 1152
Fax:(+41-629) 62 1160
email: info@spycher-handwerk.ch
www.spycher-handwerk.ch

TAIWAN:
Founder Tek Intíl Co Ltd
Taipei
Tel:(+886-2) 2-781 1699
Fax:(+886-2) 2-751 2521
email: foundtwn@ms12.hinet.net
www.foundertek.com.tw

UNITED KINGDOM:
Frank Herring & Sons
Dorset
Tel:(+44-1305) 264449
Fax:(+44-1305) 250675
email: info@frankherringandsons.com
www.frankherringandsons.com

UNITED STATES:
Foxglove Fiberarts Supply
Bainbridge Island, Washington
Tel:(+1-206) 780-2747
Fax:(+1-206) 780-2848
email: sales@foxglovefiber.com
www.foxglovefiber.com

If your country is not listed
here please write to:
Ashford Handicrafts Ltd
PO Box 474
Ashburton
New Zealand
Tel: +64 3 308 9087
Fax: +64 3 308 8664
Email: sales@ashford.co.nz